LOCKE'S *ESSAY CONCERNING HUMAN UNDERSTANDING*

A Reader's Guide

WILLIAM UZGALIS

continuum

Continuum International Publishing Group
The Tower Building   80 Maiden Lane
11 York Road   Suite 704
London   New York
SE1 7NX   NY 10038

British Library Cataloguing-in-Publication Data
A catalogue record for this book is available from the British Library.

ISBN: HB: 0–8264–9032–8
9780826490322
PB: 0–8264–9033–6
9780826490339

Library of Congress Cataloging-in-Publication Data
Uzgalis, W.
Locke's Essay Concerning Human Understanding : a reader's guide / by
William Uzgalis.
p. cm.
Includes bibliographical references.
ISBN-13: 978–0–8264–9032–2
ISBN-10: 0–8264–9032–8
ISBN-13: 978–0–8264–9033–9
ISBN-10: 0–8264–9033–6
1. Locke, John, 1632–1704. Essay concerning human understanding. 2.
Knowledge, Theory of. I. Title.

B1294.U95 2007
121 - -dc22

2006033297

Typeset by YHT Ltd, London
Printed and bound in Great Britain by
MPG Books Ltd, Bodmin, Cornwall

WITHDRAWN

CONTENTS

CHAPTER 1

CONTEXT

John Locke (1632–1704) was an English philosopher, Oxford don, doctor, political and economic researcher, political operative, colonial administrator and revolutionary. Locke's *An Essay Concerning Human Understanding* (1689) established him as one of the greatest philosophers of the modern period. Locke grew up and lived through one of the most extraordinary centuries of English political and intellectual history. It was a century in which conflicts between crown and parliament and the overlapping conflicts between Protestants, Anglicans and Catholics swirled into civil war in the 1640s. With the defeat and death of Charles I in the civil war, there began a great experiment in government institutions including the abolition of the monarchy, the House of Lords and the Anglican Church, and the creation of Oliver Cromwell's Protectorate in the 1650s. The restoration of Charles II in 1660 occurred after the collapse of the Protectorate in 1658, after the death of Cromwell and the failure of his son. The return of the monarchy brought with it the re-establishment of the House of Lords and the Anglican Church. This period lasted from 1660 to 1688. It was marked by continued conflicts between king and parliament and debates over religious toleration for Protestant nonconformists and Catholics. This period ends with the Glorious Revolution of 1688 in which James II was driven from England and replaced by William of Orange and his wife Mary. This tumultuous political period also saw the founding of the Royal Society and the development of a rich scientific culture in England, nourished by such notable figures as Robert Boyle, Isaac Newton and Robert Hooke among others.

John Locke was born in Wrighton, Somerset on 28 August 1632 into a family of very minor gentry. His father owned some houses in and around Pensford, a small town near Bristol, practised law and held some minor local administrative positions. When the English Civil War broke out, Locke's father served as a captain in a local cavalry regiment in one of the parliamentary armies. The regiment was commanded by Alexander Popham, a much more senior figure among the Somerset gentry than Locke's father. The parliamentary army under Waller was defeated at the battle of Devizes in July of 1643 and the regiment subsequently dispersed.

Locke senior's association with Alexander Popham proved to be enormously important for the education of the young John Locke. Popham became the Member of Parliament for Bath and could recommend boys for places at Westminster, then the best school in England. He recommended Locke and Locke entered Westminster in 1647, where he mainly studied Greek, Latin and Hebrew. Westminster School was connected with Christ Church, Oxford and Locke obtained one of the three scholarships for boys from Westminster and took up residence at Oxford in the autumn of 1652.

Locke's time at Oxford represents the second stage in his life. The curriculum was dominated by the Scholastic and Aristotelian doctrines and methods of disputation that had so exasperated a young Thomas Hobbes fifty years earlier. Locke came to detest the method of scholastic disputation and its associated model of science. One of the themes of *An Essay Concerning Human Understanding* is the rejection of this model of science in favour of an empiricist model. Nonetheless, Locke fulfilled the requirements for his B.A. degree in 1657, and an M.A. followed in 1658.

Locke needed to decide on a career. The great majority of Oxford graduates were ordained as priests. Locke's father may have had a career in the church in mind for his son. Eventually, however, Locke decided against ordination. This left medicine as Locke's most likely career choice. He apparently began exploring medicine in earnest in the late 1650s. There was a vigorous group at Oxford advocating the empirical study of medicine. Locke joined this group and the study of medicine eventually led to an interest in natural philosophy and chemistry. He met Robert Boyle some time around 1660. Boyle was a chemist who had done work with the vacuum pump and was the leader of a group at Oxford advocating the new mechanical and corpuscularian philosophy. After the Restoration, this group left Oxford for London and formed the Royal Society. It was in the early 1660s that Locke began reading Boyle's work on the air pump and Descartes' scientific and philosophical works.

The Restoration of Charles II to the English throne and the establishment of an authoritarian government led Locke to read Anglican theology and to engage in polemics against both Catholics and Protestant nonconformists. He wrote two treatises arguing that the leader of the state has the right to determine the form of religious worship for all. J.R. Milton argues on this basis that Locke in the early 1660s was largely an orthodox Anglican. Locke would hardly have 'advocated a policy requiring the imposition of a religious orthodoxy he himself did not accept' (Milton: 7). Locke was well regarded by the university and was appointed to a series of offices in the 1660s.

He might well have remained at Oxford had he not met Lord Ashley, one of the richest men in England, in the summer of 1666. Ashley was not well and came to Oxford to take the medicinal waters. He met Locke and they liked one another. He invited Locke to London as his personal physician; Locke accepted the offer and moved to London the following year. Thus began the third stage of Locke's life.

In London, Locke stayed at Lord Ashley's residence, Exeter House, and in 1668 supervized a successful operation on a cyst on Lord Ashley's liver that undoubtedly saved his life. The family gave Locke all the credit for his patient's remarkable survival. As Ashley was a member of the government, Locke not only served as a physician but as an economic researcher and secretary of the Board of Trade and Plantations. Ashley became the financier in a plan to establish English colonies in the Carolinas and Locke served as the secretary to the Lords Proprietors of the Carolinas, and participated in the writing of the Fundamental Constitutions of the Carolinas.

In 1671 there was a meeting in Locke's rooms in Exeter House that Locke describes as the occasion that gave rise to the writing of *An Essay Concerning Human Understanding*. The discussions raised issues about the limits of human understanding in respect to morality and revealed religion. Determining the limits of human understanding became the main project of the *Essay*. Locke was also responding to the Renaissance sceptics who denied that any knowledge is possible, as well as Descartes and his followers who claimed that reason provided fundamental and substantive truths about God, our own nature and the physical universe.

Lord Ashley became Lord Chancellor of England in 1672 and at that point was made the First Earl of Shaftesbury. Shaftesbury eventually had a falling out with the king (who probably never trusted him since he had been part of the Commonwealth government). He was dismissed as Lord Chancellor in 1673 and became the leader of the opposition to the government. In 1675 Locke went to France where he remained for three-and-a-half years. Locke learned French and met prominent followers of both Descartes and Gassendi. He continued to work on the *Essay* during this period.

Locke returned to England in May 1679. The country was in the throes of a political crisis. The popish plot (a bogus plot to kill King Charles and replace him with his Catholic brother) had stirred up anti-Catholic sentiment. Shaftesbury and his party were attempting to exclude James Duke of York, an avowed Catholic, from succeeding his brother to the throne of England. Charles avoided one exclusion bill by dissolving parliament, but a second failed in the House of Lords. When a third exclusion bill failed because Charles dissolved the Oxford parliament of 1681 before the bill could even make its way through the House of Commons, many of the Whig party gave up and went home, while the more radical element led by Shaftesbury began seriously considering revolution. It was in this context that Locke wrote the *Two Treatises of Government*. Charles was determined to crush Shaftesbury and eventually Shaftesbury went into hiding. When a proposed plot to kill the king and his brother failed to materialize, Shaftesbury escaped to Holland where he died in January 1683. The Rye House plot to kill the king and his brother was betrayed and the government started arresting people in June 1683. Locke left London for the West Country a week before the arrests began, put his affairs in order and left for exile in Holland in September 1683.

During his exile in Holland Locke was both actively involved with the exiled English revolutionary movement and working on *An Essay Concerning Human Understanding*. He worked on it from the winter of 1683 until 1686 when it reached pretty much its final form. He sent several partial drafts back to England. He interrupted work on the *Essay* to write the *Letter Concerning Toleration* during the winter of 1685–6; that work was published anonymously a few months after Locke returned to England. While Locke had an ongoing interest in religious toleration in the English context, this work may have been inspired by the revocation of the Edict of Nantes by Louis XIV in 1685, after which Protestant refugees began pouring across the French border into Holland. It is in this work that Locke advocates the separation of church and state.

While Locke was living in exile in Holland, Charles II died in 1685 and was succeeded by his brother James. James II alienated much of his support and this led William of Orange to cross the Channel in 1688 with an army. Upon William's landing, James realized that resistance was futile and fled to France. With the Glorious Revolution of 1688, as it came to be called, it was safe for Locke to return to England. He came back aboard the royal yacht bringing Princess Mary to join her husband.

With his return to England, Locke began preparing his two chief works for publication. The *Two Treatises of Government* appeared in October 1689 and *An Essay Concerning Human Understanding* at the beginning of December 1689. Both works were published before the 1690 date on their title pages. The *Essay* was published under Locke's own name while the *Two Treatises* was published anonymously. An English translation of the *Letter Concerning Toleration* was also published that year (Locke, 1823, Vol. VI: 1–58).

An Essay Concerning Human Understanding is Locke's *magnum opus*. It established his reputation as one of the greatest philosophers of his age. It is, as Peter Nidditch, the editor of the best critical edition of the *Essay* says: 'the primary classic of systematic empiricism'. It is, as he goes on to say: 'the vital ancestor of all later Empiricism . . .' (Locke, 1972: ix). Over the next fourteen years there were four editions of the *Essay* and a fifth shortly after Locke's death in 1704. There were substantive changes between the first and second editions and between the third and fourth. All of the changes to the various editions are noted in Peter Nidditch's fine edition of *An Essay Concerning Human Understanding* issued by the Clarendon Press in 1972. The citations to the *Essay* in this book all refer to that edition, though the Book, chapter and section numbers should make it easy enough to find the passages referred to below in other editions of the *Essay*. After the publication of the *Essay*, Locke rarely responded to his critics, though he made an exception for Bishop Edward Stillingfleet. The bishop raised a variety of objections to Locke's philosophy, charging that the new 'way of ideas' would lead to scepticism, along with a variety of other perceptive complaints. Locke answered Stillingfleet at length (Locke's side is itself longer than the *Essay*). In some editions of the *Essay*, portions of the Locke/Stillingfleet correspondence are included.

There are, in this Reader's Guide, occasional references to the correspondence where it clarifies the meaning of the *Essay*.

By 1700 Locke had retired from government service and remained in the country at Oates in the family house of Damaris and Sir Francis Masham until his death in 1704. He continued to revise his works for publication until just before his death.

CHAPTER 2

OVERVIEW OF THEMES

Locke's *Essay* is 721 pages long in the Nidditch edition and deals with a number of important issues, primarily in metaphysics and epistemology, though these often have wider implications relating to religion, morality and politics.

Locke offers the *Essay* in part as a way of dealing with sceptics by determining the scope and limits of human understanding. He is also developing in detail an empiricist programme that will remove scholastic and rationalist 'rubbish' and make it easier for us to acquire knowledge. In this respect he sees himself as an 'under-labourer' to the great scientists of the era. There is, however, a serious tension between Locke's empiricism with its emphasis on experience as providing the evidential basis for knowledge and the corpuscular philosophy or atomism which offer explanations in terms of particles of which we have no experience. Still, Locke is certainly not, like Berkeley, a conservative religionist who uses empiricism to oppose the scientific achievements of the 17th century.

In Book I of the *Essay*, Locke discusses and refutes the doctrine that there are innate principles and ideas, either speculative or practical. This rejection of innate ideas has anti-authoritarian implications for religion, philosophy, morality and politics. In Book II of the *Essay*, Locke gives his positive account of the origin of ideas – all of our ideas are ultimately derived from experience, either from sensation or reflection. Some notable themes in Book II include the nature of our ideas of bodies, free will and volition, and personal identity. In Book III Locke discusses language and its relation to knowledge. There are issues about the nature of essences and classification, abstraction, natural kinds, substances and modes as well as proposals for dealing with the imperfections and abuses of language. In Book IV he defines knowledge, talks about grades of knowledge, kinds of knowledge, the limits of knowledge, probability and the relation of faith and reason. Of particular interest are issues about materialism, God's existence and the relation of faith to reason.

One might count among the important themes running through the *Essay* the central role of reason and inquiry in achieving human maturity, autonomy, freedom and happiness. This stress on the development of one's reasoning abilities connects in important ways with Locke's anti-authoritarianism and his advocacy of a rational religion. Locke's discussion of free will and determinism (in Book II, chapter XXI) and his view of personal identity (in Book II, chapter XXVII) and ethics (Book II, chapter XXVIII) are important elements connected with this theme and are among the most interesting sections in the book.

There is one issue that raises perhaps the most important interpretative problem in the whole essay and culminates in the discussion of real knowledge in Book IV. The issue (which shows up in different forms in Books II, III and IV is whether we can ever get outside the circle of our own experience to know anything about things outside ourselves. Locke's response to scepticism is a connected theme.

CHAPTER 3

READING THE TEXT

THE EPISTLE TO THE READER

John Locke's *An Essay Concerning Human Understanding* begins with 'The Epistle to the Reader'. In the Epistle he gives the reader a little information about how the *Essay* came to be written and how the reader should read it:

> Were it fit to trouble thee with the History of this Essay, I should tell thee that five or six Friends meeting at my Chamber, and discoursing on a Subject very remote from this, found themselves quickly at a stand, by the Difficulties that rose on every side. After we had a while puzzled our selves, without coming any nearer a Resolution of those Doubts that perplexed us, it came into my Thoughts, that we took a wrong course; and that, before we set ourselves on Enquiries of that Nature, it was necessary to examine our own Abilities, and see, what Objects our Understandings were, or were not fitted to deal with. This I proposed to the Company, who all readily assented; and thereupon it was agreed, that this should be our first Enquiry. ('The Epistle': 7)

He produced some 'hasty and undigested Thoughts' for the next meeting and these

> gave the first entrance into this Discourse, which having thus begun by Chance, was continued by Intreaty; written by incoherent parcels; and after long intervals of neglect, resum'd again as my Humour or Occasions permitted; and at last, in a retirement, where an Attendance on my Health gave me leisure, it was brought into that order, thou now seest it. ('The Epistle': 7)

One of Locke's friends at this meeting, James Tyrell, noted in his copy of the *Essay* that he had attended the meeting that Locke mentions and that it was issues about morality and revealed religion that puzzled them.

This story gives us one of the keys to explaining why Locke's *Essay* was such a success from the beginning. John Yolton notes:

> Besides his style, another important factor accounting for Locke's popularity was the way in which he oriented his discussions around the religious and moral questions of great significance to the majority of people in the seventeenth century. Non-epistemological questions served as the stimulus for the discussion of problems of knowledge. It should have been no surprise to Locke to find his doctrines taken as applying to the context from which they originated. Those who had the keenest interest in his book were theologians and moralists concerned with seeing what good or harm its principles would involve for their values. The seventeenth century was marked by a strong interest in science, but the interests of religion and morality were still paramount in men's minds. Thus Locke's concern to solve problems of knowledge for the sake of those values went along with his literary style and fluency to give his book a wide popularity. (Yolton, 1996: 21–2)

In the twentieth century we have learned a good deal more about the composition of the *Essay*, because Paul Mellon purchased the Lovelace papers and donated them to Oxford University. These papers contained, amongst other things, several drafts of the *Essay*. These early drafts have now been published and scholars have begun tracing the development of Locke's ideas through these first drafts.

In telling the story of its genesis, Locke announces the aim of the *Essay*: to try to determine what objects our understanding is or is not fitted to deal with before we engage in an effort to find particular truths about particular subjects. Locke thinks that if we do not do this, we will find ourselves like him and his friends, at a stand (unable to proceed with our enquiries) and without any resolution of our difficulties. While issues about morality and religion may have made the essay popular, Locke's interest in science and its connection with knowledge also plays a prominent role in the *Essay*. In another famous passage, Locke tells the reader that:

The Commonwealth of Learning is not, at this time without Master-Builders; whose mighty Designs, in advancing the Sciences, will leave lasting Monuments to the Admiration of Posterity; But Everyone must not hope to be a Boyle, or a Sydenham; and in an age that produces such Masters, as the great ... Huygenius, and the incomparable Mr. Newton, with some other of that strain; 'tis Ambition enough to be employed as an Under-Labourer in clearing Ground a little, and removing some of the Rubbish, that lies in the way of Knowledge ... ('The Epistle': 9–10, 34–5).

Locke is treating his work as standing three steps below the scientific work of Huygens and Newton, Boyle and Sydenham. He is a humble remover of intellectual rubbish. It turns out that it is mainly the Aristotelian/scholastic philosophy then taught in the universities that he regards as rubbish. Locke remarks that knowledge would have been much more advanced '... if the Endeavours of ingenious and industrious Men had not been much cumbred with the learned but frivolous use of uncouth, affected or unintelligible Terms, introduced into the Sciences ...' ('The Epistle': 10). He continues:

Vague and insignificant Forms of Speech, and Abuse of Language, have so long passed for Mysteries of Science; and Hard or misapply'd Words, with little or no meaning, have by such Prescription, such a Right to be mistaken for deep Learning, and height of Speculation, that it will not be easie to persuade, either those who speak, or those who hear them, that they are but the Covers of Ignorance, and hindrance of true Knowledge. ('The Epistle': 10, 11–17).

So, here we find Locke joining the revolt against the Aristotelian/scholastic education in the universities along with not just the scientists of the Royal Society but also many other European thinkers of the period, including Bacon, Hobbes and Descartes. It turns out that while Locke has a much higher opinion of Descartes than he does of the scholastics, there are a number of important aspects of Descartes' philosophy about God, minds and bodies that Locke does not accept. Another point that Locke makes which is worth noting is that much of the rubbish removal will come in Book III of the *Essay*.

As we shall see from the Introduction, Locke's labours really involve considerably more than just removing scholastic intellectual rubbish and Cartesian mistakes. He is, amongst other things, providing us with an account of our own abilities and powers, pointing out our modest station in the vastness of the universe and describing the role of reason and inquiry in the full development of the individual, along with human flourishing in this life and for the next. It is as Hans Aarsleff calls it: 'an education to humanity' (Aarsleff, 1994: 260). This suggests greater ambitions than the modest title of mere under-labourer might suggest.

BOOK I OF THE *ESSAY*

The Introduction

A natural history of ideas

In section 2 of the Introduction to the *Essay*, Locke tells us that his method is going to be a historical plain method (see I. I. 2. 4–8.: 44). What does Locke have in mind when he talks of 'this Historical, plain method'? It appears that what Locke is concerned with is giving an account of the origin of 'those Notions of Things we have.' He says later (in section 3 of the Introduction):

> *First*, I shall enquire into the *Original* of those *Ideas*, Notions, or whatever else you please to call them, which a Man observes, and is conscious to himself he has in his Mind; and the ways whereby the Understanding comes to be furnished with them. (I. I. 3. 22–25.: 44)

So, the project is to find out how we come to have the ideas that we observe ourselves to have in our minds. This will provide the basis for determining 'what *Knowledge* the Understanding hath by those *Ideas*; and the Certainty, Evidence and Extent of it' (I. I. 3. 26–28.: 44).

Still, where did Locke get the idea of the historical plain method? Locke was a member of a scientific group at Oxford led by Robert Boyle. After the Restoration this group was responsible for founding the Royal Society in London and Locke was one of its early members. Scholars have intensively studied the scientific programme of the Royal Society. One line was derived from Bacon and involved the collection of facts through observation and experiment. Another was the acceptance of the mechanical philosophy and the corpuscular hypothesis regarding matter. John Yolton, in *Locke and the Compass of Human Understanding*, claims that observation and the making of natural histories was even more fundamental to the science of the Royal Society than was acceptance of the corpuscular hypothesis (Yolton, 1970: 7–8). As Yolton says: 'In the minds of seventeenth century writers on science, there was a distinction between the mechanical and the experimental philosophies. The latter was the method for getting data, compiling histories of phenomena' (Yolton, 1970: 6). He goes on to remark that in the seventeenth century lack of sufficient data was the factor most responsible for fallacious reasoning. Hence the importance of observation and the heaping up of facts that Bacon had advocated. Locke's interest in the historical plain method probably comes more directly from the physician Thomas Sydenham: in the late 1660s Locke was collaborating with Sydenham. In Locke's papers is a work in his own hand entitled *De Arte Medica*, which advocates an empirical approach to medical practice while expressing a profound scepticism about hypotheses concerning the nature of disease (Milton: 9). Locke remained closer to Boyle and the corpuscularians than to Sydenham, but still he was sceptical about the possibility of providing corpuscular explanations of particular bodies.

What is remarkable about Locke's project is that he is applying the techniques of medicine and natural philosophy to the human mind. By discovering how we acquire ideas and what ideas are acquired, Locke thinks we can determine what knowledge we can have and what the limits of the human understanding are. While Books I and II are clearly concerned with the genetic account of the origin of ideas, presumably Books III and IV, which deal with ideas as expressed in language, and knowledge and probability respectively, represent distinct stages in the natural history of the understanding.

The project of the essay

Improving human life and flourishing

Locke's philosophy is essentially optimistic about the possibility of progress towards human flourishing. He sees human beings as limited, finite beings in respect to knowledge; but we should not be distressed by our limitations. He writes: 'For though the

Comprehension of our Understanding, comes exceeding short of the vast Extent of Things; yet we shall have cause enough to magnify the Bountiful Author of our Being, for that Portion and Degree of Knowledge, he has bestowed upon us, so far above all the rest of the Inhabitants of this our Mansion' (I. I. 5. 15–19.: 45). He goes on to say that God has provided us with 'Whatsoever is necessary for the Conveniences of Life, and the Information of Vertue; and has put within the reach of their Discovery the comfortable Provision for this Life and the Way that leads to a Better' (I. I. 5. 20–25.: 45). Empirical inquiry, on Locke's view, moves us towards human flourishing both in the sense that it will lead to 'the comfortable Provision for this Life,' but also in the sense that it makes the individual free from having to believe others without evidence. There is an anti-authoritarian streak running through Locke's philosophy that is most prominent in his political works, but which also shows up in his view of the value of inquiry and his rejection of innate ideas. Inquiry and the use of reason are the keys to genuine freedom and human maturity,

Establishing the limits of the understanding

Locke sees human understanding as finite. One of the chief aims of the *Essay* is to try to determine what the boundaries of the human understanding are. Locke thinks that establishing these boundaries will have both practical and epistemic benefits. It also represents an effort to attain the knowledge necessary to direct the conduct of human life (I. I. 6. 27–32.: 46). Locke also thinks that establishing the bounds of human understanding will aid inquiry in some areas (by convincing us that this lies within the boundaries of what we can understand) and will diminish scepticism (see I. I. 7. 1–23.: 47). Locke thinks that scepticism arises when we are ignorant of the bounds of human understanding and is likely to diminish when we banish such ignorance. The marks of going beyond our powers of comprehension are that we raise questions we cannot answer and multiply disputes that cannot be resolved. (Compare this passage with Locke's account in the 'Epistle to the Reader' of the meeting in his rooms that gave rise to the *Essay*). Presumably questions that are within our capacity to answer we can, in the end, answer.

The search for the boundaries of human understanding can be found in the great French philosopher René Descartes. Descartes' project is to try to determine what can be known and what cannot.

Locke, however, is more explicit about the whole range of the project; it is not just knowledge, but probability and faith that interest him. This effort to try to find the boundaries of human understanding becomes an influential theme in European philosophy; one can see it at work in Berkeley and Hume. Central to Kant's philosophy is the exploration of what truths can be known by reason (the *synthetic a priori* truths) and which of the claims to be known by reason are illegitimate. In the Antimonies section of the *Critique of Pure Reason* he spells out what the signs are that inquiry has gone beyond the bounds of human understanding. In this he is the heir of Descartes, but more particularly of Locke and Hume. Contemporary philosophers still wrestle with this issue.

Innate principles: a false origin of ideas

The purpose of the remainder of Book I of the *Essay* is negative. Locke takes up and examines the claim that our speculative and moral principles are built into the mind. The claim, as he understands it, is that these principles are innate or present at birth. Locke's purpose is to show that this is false. Why Locke places this attack on innate principles right at the beginning of the *Essay* is puzzling. Why didn't he begin with his own positive empiricist programme? Margaret Atherton has suggested that the traditional interpretation of the relation between Locke's empiricism and his attack on innate ideas gets the order of his argument wrong in suggesting that his rejection of innateness is a consequence of his empiricism. On her view 'Locke's demonstration of where our ideas come from depends upon his rejection of the possibility of innateness, which in turn, stems from a picture of what mentality is like and what mental states consist in.' (Atherton: 48). We will take up the issue of mental states when we examine Locke's arguments.

In Book I Locke does not give us the names of the advocates of innate principles and ideas whom he is attacking. Scholars have offered a range of possible targets, including Descartes, the Cambridge Platonists, scholastic philosophers and enthusiastic sectarians in religion and politics. There is even the suggestion that Locke had no one in mind and that he is constructing a position to refute. John Yolton has shown quite convincingly that there was a considerable literature in seventeenth-century England that used the language of innate principles to try to preserve religious and moral beliefs.

It is clear from the *Essay* that Locke's attack on innate principles and ideas had an anti-authoritarian element to it. Looking at the transition from Book I to Book II we find Locke talking about the uses of innate ideas to control and govern those who accept them (see I. IV. 24. 32–10.: 101–2). This passage suggests that those who teach the doctrine of innate ideas that Locke is concerned about use the doctrine to stop inquiry and questioning and to gain control over the minds of others. Locke's anti-authoritarianism and his vision of inquiry as the way to acquire truth and knowledge are clearly connected here. To inquire requires that one use one's own reason and judgement. To do this is to realize human potential. This language of 'masters and teachers' also suggests that Locke sees the scholastic curriculum of the universities as blocking rational inquiry. In Book IV, chapter VII, section 10, pp. 596–7, Locke connects the scholastic model of science as reasoning from first principles to the rest of knowledge with the doctrine of innate principles. In Book IV, chapter XVII he argues that the syllogistic logic is of little use in the discovery of truths. Thus, Locke rejects the Scholastic model of science, the scholastic claim that principles are innate, and the syllogistic logic that the scholastics used to argue from innate first principles to the rest of knowledge.

We know that Locke was concerned about philosophers who argued on behalf of innate principles. In Book II, chapter I, sections 9–20, Locke attacks Descartes' doctrine that the soul is a thinking thing (*sum res cogitans*). It is plain that he sees this doctrine as implying that the soul has innate ideas. Locke also wrote a long '*Examination of the Opinions of P. Malebranche in seeing all Things in God*' (Locke, 1823, Vol. IX), which he originally intended to add to the *Essay*, but which was eventually published separately. A good part of Locke's objection to Malebranche and his English followers, such as John Norris, concerned the advocacy of innate ideas. In Book IV Locke links the scholastic and Aristotelian philosophers with innate ideas (see IV. VII. 3. 11–33.: 600). In Book IV, chapter 12, section 4, Locke lists a whole series of ancient philosophers with false principles in both natural philosophy and morality. This gives us a good set of examples of how students might be influenced by accepting certain principles as innate.

The arguments against innate principles and ideas

In his account of the use of innate principles in the seventeenth century, John Yolton distinguishes two versions of the argument for innateness. First, there is a naïve version that treats innate principles as stamped on the mind at birth. The criterion for such ideas is universal consent. The second version is dispositional. On this account 'the claim for these principles being imprinted at birth was no longer included, and later, so that the name "innate" was meant to apply only to those principles that we easily assent to' (Yolton, 1996: 29). Locke attacks both versions of the doctrine.

He describes innate ideas as 'some primary notions . . . Characters as it were stamped upon the Mind of Man, which the Soul receives in its very first Being; and brings into the world with it' (I. II. 1.: 48). In pursuing this inquiry, Locke rejects the claim that there are speculative innate principles (I. II), practical innate moral principles (I. III) or that we have innate ideas of God, identity or impossibility (I. IV). Locke rejects arguments from universal assent and attacks dispositional accounts of innate principles.

Universal assent

Thus, in considering what would count as evidence from universal assent to such propositions as 'What is, is' or 'It is impossible for the same thing to be and not to be' he holds that children and idiots should be aware of such truths if they were innate but that they 'have not the least Apprehension or Thought of them' (I. II. 5. 27–28.: 49). Why should children and idiots be aware of and be able to articulate such propositions? Locke says that it seems to him 'near a Contradiction, to say, that there are Truths imprinted on the Soul, which it perceives or understands not; imprinting, if it signify anything, being nothing else but the making certain Truths to be perceived.' (I. II. 5. 30–34.: 49). So, Locke's first point is that if propositions were innate, infants and idiots (and indeed everyone else) should immediately perceive them, but there is no evidence that they do so.

Here we have the first appearance of Locke's views about mental states. Scholars have complained that this account of innate ideas is a straw man, but Yolton, as we have seen, has shown that this is not the case. Still, this is the naïve view. In criticizing it Locke seems to be committed to the claim that having innate ideas requires that we be conscious of them. Margaret Atherton notes that 'Locke's attitude with respect to innateness depends so heavily on his perception of a strong connection between "being in the mind" and "being in consciousness" that it has sometimes been overlooked, in part, perhaps, because such a view seems to be quite unnaturally restrictive' (Atherton: 51). She goes on to argue that Locke does hold this view, but that he does not need to be saved from what seem to be its most unfortunate consequences, for Locke is 'not committed to the claim that only those beliefs can be attributed to people that they happen to be consciously considering at a particular moment' (Atherton: 52). We can see the importance of this view of mental states in Locke's argument when we turn to the more sophisticated dispositional accounts of innate principles. The dispositional accounts of innate principles say, roughly, that innate propositions are capable of being perceived under certain circumstances. Until these circumstances are met the propositions remain unperceived in the mind; with the advent of these conditions, the propositions are then perceived. Locke gives an argument against innate propositions being dispositional at I. II. 5. 5–26.: 50.

The essence of this argument and many of Locke's other arguments against dispositional accounts of innate propositions is that such dispositional accounts do not provide an adequate criterion for distinguishing innate propositions from other propositions that the mind may come to discover. Thus, even if some criterion is proposed, it will turn out not to do the work it is supposed to do. For example, Locke considers the claim that innate propositions are discovered and assented to when people 'come to the use of Reason' (II. IV. 6. 8.: 51). Locke considers two possible meanings of this phrase. One is that we use reason to discover these innate propositions. Here he argues that the criterion is inadequate, because it would not distinguish axioms from theorems in mathematics (I. II. 8. 21–31.: 51). Presumably the theorems are not innate, while the axioms should be. But if both need to be discovered by reason, then there is no distinction between them. Nor will it do to say that one class (the axioms) are assented to as soon as they are perceived while the others are not. To be assented to as soon as perceived is a mark of certainty, but not of innateness. Locke also posits that truths that need to be discovered by reason could never be thought to be innate.

The second possible meaning of 'come to the use of reason' is that we discover these ideas at the time we come to use reason, but that we do not use reason to do so. He argues that this claim simply is not true. We know that children acquire such propositions before they acquire the use of reason, while others who are reasonable never acquire them (I. II. 12. 8–20.: 53).

But what, the reader may say, is Locke's positive account of innate speculative principles? What is his alternative account to that of innateness? In section 14 through 16 starting on p. 54 we get Locke's positive account of how these maxims come to be. The power to distinguish between ideas is fundamental and comes to children early. So, they quickly come to distinguish between sweet and bitter. Later they acquire language and are able to distinguish wormwood from sugar plums. Still later they may abstract such claims as the reflexivity of identity and the principle of non-contradiction where this may be useful in discourse. So, Locke's positive account of these maxims is that they are abstract general principles founded on our ability to grasp the identity of particular ideas and to distinguish one idea from another. It turns out that when Locke discusses these maxims in Book IV, he regards them as being of very little use (see IV. VII. 3.: 600).

When Locke turns from speculative principles to the question of whether there are innate practical moral principles, many of the arguments against innate speculative principles continue to apply, but there are some additional considerations. Practical principles, such as the Golden Rule, are not self-evident in the way such speculative principles as 'What is, is' are. Thus, one can clearly and sensibly ask reasons for why one should hold the Golden Rule true or obey it (I. III. 4. 1–22.: 68). There are substantial differences between people over the content of practical principles, and so they are even less likely to be innate propositions or to meet the criterion of universal assent than speculative principles.

In the fourth chapter of Book I, Locke raises similar points about the ideas that compose both speculative and practical principles. The point is that if the ideas that are constitutive of the principles are not innate, this gives us even more reason to hold that the principles are not innate. He examines the ideas of identity, impossibility and God to make these points.

Questions:

1. What are the two different theories of innateness that Locke attacks?
2. Do you find Locke's critique of the naïve theory of innate ideas compelling? Why?
3. Locke holds that all the criteria for distinguishing innate ideas from those we acquire through experience are inadequate. What makes these criteria inadequate?
4. Locke thinks that holding that there are innate practical principles is less plausible than holding that there are innate speculative principles. Why?
5. Are there versions of the innateness doctrine that Locke fails to consider? If so, what are they and how do they differ from the ones he does consider?

BOOK II OF THE *ESSAY*

The organization of Book II

Most of Book II is taken up with Locke's positive account of the origin of ideas. One might say that this is what Locke is doing in the first 28 chapters of Book II. In chapters XXIX through XXXII he turns to judgements we make about ideas such as whether they are clear and distinct or obscure and confused; and finally in chapter XXXIII (added to the fourth edition of the *Essay*) he discusses the association of ideas. This account of the organization of Book II does not reveal the extent to which Locke is dealing with substantive problems in philosophy in the course of explaining the origin of various ideas. He has much of interest to say about the nature of material bodies and minds, the nature of voluntary action and disputes about free will and determinism, identity and personal identity and various other topics.

If we try to map these particular topics we can sometimes find that they are encompassed in a single chapter and sometimes not. As to material bodies, Locke talks about solidity in chapter IV. He makes the distinction between primary and secondary qualities of bodies in chapter VIII and deals with concepts that are closely connected with material bodies, such as number, infinity, space and time in chapters XIII through XVII. Issues about voluntary action and free will and determinism are taken up in chapter XXI, entitled

'Of Power.' Chapter XXVII deals with issues about identity and personal identity.

Empiricism and ideas

The origin of ideas in sensation and reflection

Locke begins chapter I of Book II by claiming that everyone is conscious that he thinks and that while he is thinking the objects of thinking are ideas, so "'tis past doubt that Men have in their Minds several *Ideas*, such as are those expressed by the words, *Whiteness, Hardness, Sweetness, Thinking, Motion, Man, Elephant, Army, Drunkenness*, and others' (II. I. 1. 4–6.: 104). If the question is then asked, how does a man come by these ideas, Locke notes that 'I know it is received Doctrine, that men have native *Ideas*, and original Characters stamped upon their Minds, in their very first Being' (II. I. 1. 7–9.: 104). Locke notes that his rejection of this doctrine in the first book of the *Essay* will be more easily accepted when he has explained whence the understanding gets all the ideas it has. He intends to base this on everyone's observation and experience.

He begins by supposing that the mind is 'white Paper, void of all Characters, without any *Ideas*; How comes it to be furnished? Whence comes it by that vast store, which the busy and boundless Fancy of Man has painted on it, with an almost endless variety? Whence has it all the materials of Reason and Knowledge?' (II. I. 2. 17–19.: 104). The answer he proposes is that all of these materials come from experience. But what is experience? Locke's answer is that experience consists either in ideas about external objects we get from the senses, or ideas about the internal operations of our own minds. 'These two are the Fountains of Knowledge, from whence all the *Ideas* we have, or can naturally have, do spring' (II. I. 2. 25–6.: 104). Locke will call the first of these 'sensation' and the second 'reflection'. Presuming that these are the origins of all our ideas, we would have no need for the hypothesis of innate ideas.

Both of these categories of experience are problematic. Sensation is problematic for a number of reasons. One reason has to do with sceptical challenges to what we can know about the external world, along with issues about what kind of theory of perception Locke holds. These issues turn out to be central to interpreting the *Essay* as a whole, so it is worth noting how Locke begins his account of sensation (see II. I. 3. 1–8.: 105). Locke assumes that there are objects external to us that we can sense (if only indirectly), that there is a process of sensation and that this process ends by producing perceptions in the mind of qualities like yellow, heat and so on. This may all seem quite obvious. But, this is true only if one is unfamiliar with the powerful challenges to knowledge offered by Renaissance scepticism. Michel de Montaigne, the greatest of the French Renaissance sceptics, in *An Apology for Raimond Sebond*, argues that perception gives us only subjective opinion and not knowledge. The sceptical challenge was taken up in different ways in various countries and at different times. It is worth noting briefly that in his *Meditations on First Philosophy* Descartes begins by setting aside the senses as reliable sources of knowledge and specifically rejects the claim that we know that there are objects outside ourselves that cause the ideas in us. Descartes later offers proofs that there are such objects, but takes scepticism towards the senses far more seriously than Locke.

Locke goes on to take up the nature of reflection (see II. I. 4. 11–24.: 105). He calls this process 'reflection', because when we perceive or doubt, we are conscious that we are engaged in such an activity; our awareness that we are doing x reflects, as it were, x. In the chapter on identity and personal identity added to the second edition he is quite explicit about this. In defining a person he says that persons know themselves to be themselves at different times and places by consciousness 'which is inseparable from thinking, and as it seems to me essential to it: It being impossible for anyone to perceive, without perceiving that he does perceive' (II. XXVII. 9. 13–16.: 335). Locke's view, then, is that any act of thinking carries a reflective act of conscious awareness along with it. This amounts to an act of inner sense. So, reflection is the way in which the mind comes to have ideas about its own operations. This account of reflection may again seem extraordinarily obvious. But there are many issues that arise from it suggesting it is not. For example, what exactly is the inner organ that allows us to view the operations of our own minds? How accurate is it?

In section 6 Locke notes that we have little reason to think that a child at his arrival into the world has plenty of ideas 'that are to be the matter of his future Knowledge.' Here presumably we have the plain, historical method at work. He wants us to consider what we are like in respect to ideas when we first come into the world. Locke claims that we are quickly affected by the bodies about us; colours and tastes crowd in upon us 'before the Memory begins to keep the Register of Time and Order' but ''tis often so late, before some unusual qualities come in the way, that there are few Men that cannot recollect the beginning of their Acquaintance with them ...' (II. I. 6. 26–29.: 106). The taste of pineapple is one of those unusual tastes that one might come upon so late that one would remember the encounter.

Locke notes parallels and differences between sensation and reflection. He tells us that reflection requires attention to the operations of the mind in order to acquire clear and distinct ideas about such operations, just as sensation requires attention to gain clear and distinct ideas of landscapes and the parts of clocks (II. I. 7. 8–22.: 107). Children tend to be drawn towards the external world and are 'apt to be delighted with the variety of changing Objects' (II. I. 8. 33–1.: 107–8). So, people 'growing up in a constant attention to Outward Sensations, seldom make any considerable Reflection on what passes within them, till they come to be of riper Years; and some scarce never at all' (II. I. 8. 4–7.: 108).

In sections 9–20 of chapter I Locke digresses from his task of accounting for the origin of ideas to attack the hypothesis of the Cartesians that the soul always thinks and that the soul is essentially a thinking thing. Here we get the connection between Descartes' account of the soul and the innate principles and ideas hypothesis Locke attacked in Book I (see II. I. 9. 8–16.: 108).

This passage strongly suggests that Locke sees Descartes' claim in 'Meditation II' that his essence is a thinking thing as entailing a commitment to innate ideas. For if his essence is to think, then he must think as soon as that self is created and the object of his thought must be ideas, and all of this must happen before birth, thus entailing a commitment to innate ideas. Locke's attack on the Cartesian *sum res cogitans* in these sections foreshadows much of his most interesting work on personal identity in II. XXVII.

Locke disputes the claim that the soul is always thinking. He argues that experience should be the judge of the issue and that it is a matter of fact that needs to be determined. In his arguments we find, once again, the strong connection between thinking and consciousness that Margaret Atherton found in Book I of the *Essay*. Locke says: 'I do say, he cannot think at any time waking or sleeping without being sensible of it. Our being sensible of it is not necessary to any thing, but to our thoughts; and to them it is; and to them it will always be necessary, till we can think without being conscious of it' (II. I. 10. 26–30.: 109). Locke argues that thinking is an operation of the mind just as motion is an operation of the body and just as the body need not always be in motion, so the soul need not always be thinking. In sleep, when we are not dreaming, we presumably are not thinking.

In sections 20–22 Locke returns to tracing the acquisition of ideas of a child from the womb through its development of ideas of reflection. Sections 23 and 24 are a summary of the conclusions of the chapter about sensation and reflection. Section 25 makes the point that in its reception of the ideas of sensation the mind is passive. Locke remarks: 'These *simple Ideas* [of Sensation and Reflection] when offered to the mind, *the Understanding can* no more refuse to have, nor alter, when they are imprinted, nor blot them out, nor make new ones in it self, than a mirror can refuse, alter or obliterate the images or *Ideas*, which the Objects set before it, do therein produce' (II. I. 25. 24–29.: 118). This passivity of the mind in the reception of simple ideas ends up playing an important part in later arguments about the reality of knowledge in Book IV.

Questions:

1. Is the mind really passive in the way Locke claims it is?
2. If not, is this a significant problem for Locke's philosophy?
3. Does Locke's comparison of ideas in our minds to images in a mirror suggest that simple ideas are all images?

Kinds of ideas

In chapter II of Book II we get an account of simple ideas. In chapter III Locke talks about ideas derived from one sense. Chapter IV is about a particularly important idea, namely 'solidity'. Chapter V gives examples derived from several senses. Chapter VI takes up simple ideas of reflection, while chapter VII tells us about simple ideas derived from both sensation and reflection. Chapter VIII makes the distinction between ideas of primary and secondary qualities. Chapters IX–XI deal with those faculties the mind uses in dealing with ideas it gets through sensation and reflection; these faculties include perception, retention and discerning. In chapter XII Locke takes up the topic of complex ideas and then proceeds to

consider three kinds of complex ideas, modes, substances and relations. So, broadly speaking, Chapters II–XII tell us about kinds
of ideas and the faculties of the understanding that deal with them.
So we have a set of distinctions to deal with: simple and complex
ideas, ideas from one sense and several, ideas from either sensation,
or reflection, or both.

Locke begins with the distinction between simple and complex
ideas. He claims that this distinction is important in understanding
the nature, manner and extent of our knowledge. So what are
simple ideas? (see II. II. 1. 5–13.: 119). Insofar as ideas are distinct
from one another they are simple. Thus, though it is a single hand
that feels softness and warmth, and these qualities are connected in
the object, the mind distinguishes them, and so they are distinct
simple ideas (II. II. 1. 13–20.: 119). So simple ideas, whether of
sensation or reflection, have to be of one uniform appearance that
can be distinguished by the mind from other such uniform appearances and are not divisible into different ideas.

What then are complex ideas? The mind makes complex ideas
out of simple ideas by repeating, comparing and uniting them.
Thus, the mind is passive in respect of the acquisition of simple
ideas, but active in the making of complex ones. Simple ideas are
the building blocks of knowledge. In explaining the relation between the two, Locke draws an analogy between our situation in the
material world and our mental world (see II. II. 2. 3–13.: 120). This
analogy shows that Locke has an atomic theory of ideas: simple
ideas are the atoms, complex ideas the molecules. How far the
analogy can be pushed and where it might break down is a reasonable question.

The distinction between ideas derived from a single sense and
ideas derived from more than one sense goes back to Aristotle. On
Locke's account light and colours come from sight; noises, sounds
and tones from the ears; tastes and smells from nose and palate.
(These last are somewhat questionable as it turns out that taste
depends very much on smell). Locke makes the point that if a
particular sense or the nerves 'which are the Conduits, to convey
them from without to their Audience in the Brain, the Mind's
Presence-room (as I may so call it) are any of them so disordered, as
not to perform their Functions, they have no Postern to be ad-
mitted by; no other way to bring themselves into view, and be
perceived by the Understanding' (II. III. 1. 22–27.: 121). This tells

us that in Locke's view the senses are crucial to the understanding even if the mind is separate from the brain.

The next point that Locke makes is perhaps the most important in the chapter. He notes that the most considerable or numerous ideas that come from touch are heat, cold and solidity. What is important about this is that it tells us that the distinction between ideas derived from one sense and ideas derived from more than one is not equivalent to the distinction Locke is going to draw in chapter VIII between primary and secondary qualities. Heat and cold are secondary qualities, but solidity is the most important of the primary qualities. In chapter V Locke enumerates the qualities that are derived from more than one sense: extension, figure, and motion and rest of bodies. These are all primary qualities. So, the two distinctions almost but do not quite coincide.

Chapters VI and VII deal with simple ideas of reflection and simple ideas derived from both sensation and reflection. Locke tells us that perception or thinking and volition or willing are the two chief actions of the mind and these are the simple ideas of reflection. Memory, discerning, reasoning, judging, knowledge and faith are modes of these simple ideas.

Questions:

4. What makes 'thinking' and 'perception' equivalent terms?
5. Why would broad categories such as perception and volition count as simple ideas?

As for simple ideas derived from both sensation and reflection, Locke begins with pleasure and pain, remarking that: '*Delight* or *Uneasiness* one or other of them join themselves to almost all our *Ideas*, both of Sensation and Reflection' (II. VII. 2. 19–20.: 128). Pleasure and pain are, for Locke, the primary motivations to action. It is striking that emotions are here called ideas and connected with ideas that have cognitive content. We will return to this section when we take up issues about free will and determinism. The other ideas from both sensation and reflection are power, existence and unity.

Faculties for acquiring and retaining simple ideas and making complex ones

The mind receives simple ideas in the form of sensation and reflection. It uses its faculties in retaining simple ideas and making complex ideas out of its store of simple ideas. What are these faculties? Locke tells us that perception and volition are the two actions of the mind. The understanding is the power or faculty of the mind to think, while the power or faculty of volition is called the will. Remembrance, reasoning, judging, knowledge and faith are among the modes of these faculties. Locke takes up these ideas of reflection in chapters IX–XI. One feature of some interest is that Locke thinks these faculties provide the basis for distinguishing between plants and animals and between other animals and human beings.

In the chapter on perception Locke notes that perception distinguishes plants from animals. The brisk alteration of the figures and motions of plants is, he says 'bare Mechanism' (II. IX. 11. 31–34.: 147). This suggests that both animal and human perception cannot be accounted for in completely mechanical terms. This is puzzling, for in II. XXVII Locke suggests that animals and even living human bodies are very much like machines.

In the course of the chapter Locke makes some interesting points about attention to and judgement of sensations. He notes that if we are paying attention to something there are often sensations such as sounds that we fail to notice. He concludes from this that the only cases where we have '*Sense*, or *Perception*' are those where '*some* Idea *is actually produced, and present in the Understanding*' (II. IX. 4. 15–16.: 144). This suggests that Locke is familiar enough with phenomena which we might call unconscious. He is simply focusing on conscious phenomena.

William Molyneaux (1656–1698), an Irish politician and scientist, sent Locke a letter in June of 1688 in which he posed the problem of whether a man born blind who had learned to distinguish by touch a cube and a globe would be able to distinguish them simply by sight when enabled to see. Locke introduces the Molyneaux problem in the chapter on perception in order to make the point that our perception is influenced by our judgement in surprising ways and that these judgements come from experience. In the case of Molyneaux's problem, the judgement has to do with what different senses, such as sight and touch, tell us about shape. Both

Molyneaux and Locke believe that what is learned by touch, such as the difference in shape between a globe and a cube, can only be correlated with what is learned from sight by experience. The idea that such a judgement can be altered by experience conflicted with 'the traditional doctrine that the mind by reason alone (or a postulated *sensus communis*) would produce the right perception of the object without support from another sense' (Aarself: 266). The Molyneaux problem turned out to be one that attracted an enormous amount of attention both in England and on the Continent, because it raised issues in optics, geometry, theories of perception and even the physiology of the eye.

What is notably missing from Locke's account of perception is any discussion of different theories of perception. Locke's solution to the Molyneaux problem may well be an implicit criticism of the scholastic theory of perception, but this hardly counts as a sustained discussion of competing hypotheses. Locke, for example, says nothing here about representative versus naïve theories of perception. (For an account of the difference between these see the section below on 'Resemblance and Representative Theories of Perception'). Perhaps this is unsurprising. Like all ideas of reflection, he treats perception as something whose nature can be grasped by careful observation. But if there are competing theories about the nature of perception, this may well suggest that introspection alone may not be able to determine the nature of perception.

Questions:

6. What is Locke's account of perception?
7. What role does attention play in perception?
8. What is the Molyneaux problem and what is Locke's solution to it?

Retention is a concept that covers both contemplation and memory. Locke says it is 'the keeping of those simple Ideas, which from Sensation or Reflection it hath received' (II. X. 1. 20–22.: 149). Contemplation is the present awareness of an idea that has been received. Memory is the power to revive ideas that have been imprinted and then disappeared from consciousness (see II. X. 2. 3–11.: 150).

Locke's account of memory as a power to revive ideas is fine as far as it goes. But given that he says that ideas that are not perceived are nothing, it is going to be difficult for him to explain the ground of this particular power. How does one hunt up something that is nothing? The language that Locke uses to describe that additional perception that comes with memory is also of some significance. Locke says that besides the content of our memories the mind has an additional perception that 'it has had them before'. This becomes important in the debates over memory and personal identity provoked by Locke's ideas in the eighteenth century. Memory, as we shall see in II. XXVII, is crucially important to Locke's account of personal identity.

Locke proceeds to note that ideas are fixed in memory by attention and repetition and that those which make the greatest impression on us are those associated with pleasure and pain. He notes that some memories are weak and others strong. Still, there seems to be a constant decay of our ideas which requires that they be renewed by 'repeated exercise of the Senses, or Reflection on those kinds of Objects, which at first occasioned them' (II. X. 5. 28–29.: 151).

Questions:

9.   What is the difference between contemplation and memory?
10   What is Locke's account of personal memory?

Discerning is the ability to tell ideas apart, to distinguish them. To fail to discern is to be confused. To be able to tell apart ideas with only slight differences amounts to 'the exactness of Judgment, and the clearness of Reason, which is to be observed in one Man above another' (II. XI. 2. 18–20.: 156). Ideas when properly distinguished are clear and distinct.

Comparing ideas 'in respect to Extent, Degrees, Time, Place or any other Circumstances' produces all of the ideas of relations. Locke thinks that while it is difficult to determine how far animals partake in this faculty, this is one of those properties that distinguishes human beings from animals. 'Beasts *compare* not their *Ideas*, farther than some sensible circumstances annexed to the Objects themselves. The other power of Comparing, which may be observed in Men, belonging to general *Ideas*, and useful only to abstract Reasonings, we may probably conjecture that Beasts have not' (II. XI. 5. 35–4.: 157–8).

Composing ideas involves the mind in putting simple ideas together to form complex ones. Enlarging means repeating a single idea to get another, as multiplying a foot 5,280 times gains the concept of a mile, or repeatedly adding unities to get the whole number series. Again, Locke does not think this is an activity that animals engage in; though 'they take in and retain together several Combinations of simple *Ideas*, as possibly the Shape, Smell and Voice of his Master, make up the complex *Idea* a Dog has of him; or rather are so many distinct Marks whereby he knows him: yet I *do not* think they do of themselves ever compound them and *make complex Ideas*' (II. XI. 7. 16–20.: 158).

If composing ideas marks a clearer boundary between other animals and humans, then comparison, abstraction and the use of language make for the clearest distinction. Locke links together abstraction and the use of language. Children learn the use of signs, and 'when they have got the skill to apply the Organs of Speech to the framing of articulate Sounds, they begin to make *use of Words*, to signifie their *Ideas* to others' (II. XI. 8. 1–3.: 159). In the next section Locke describes the process of abstraction (see II. XI. 9. 7–18.: 159).

Locke thinks it clear that other animals do not use language and do not make general ideas. So, while other animals compare and compound ideas to some degree, Locke thinks that they do not engage in abstraction at all. So, a clear distinction between humans and other animals is that humans have general ideas as well as the use of language, while other animals do not. It is interesting that it is the lack of general ideas that makes the clearest distinction between other animals and humans. Locke goes on to give an example of abstraction and it is whiteness. Thus we discover that simple ideas abstracted become universals; but when one abstracts from individual things rather than their qualities, one gets the genus and species of our classificatory systems. This latter point becomes central in Book III of the *Essay*.

Questions:

11. Locke uses human powers and capacities to distinguish between humans and other animals. Does he make the distinction correctly?

12. When Locke says that dogs acquire complex ideas but do not make them, doesn't this suggest that the official doctrine that we are passive in the acquisition of simple ideas and active in the making of complex ones may not be entirely true?

Material bodies

The mechanical philosophy, corpuscles and atoms

One of the chief topics of Book II of Locke's *Essay* is the origin of our ideas of material objects. Locke is giving an empiricist account of our knowledge of material objects as well as endorsing an atomic hypothesis about the nature of bodies.

Clearly knowledge of bodies in the external world – from stars and planets to oaks, daffodils, tigers and horses, human bodies, iron, gold and so on – is of enormous importance to human self-knowledge and human flourishing. Related to our ideas of bodies are ideas of space and time. Locke is concerned both with what bodies are and what kind of knowledge we can have of material bodies. It may seem surprising that he spends so much time on these topics, but the nature of material bodies was a matter of intense controversy in the seventeenth century.

Locke's account of bodies contrasts with the Aristotelian and Cartesian accounts. He is a corpuscularian or, perhaps more precisely, an atomist. Corpuscularianism of one form or another was characteristic of the mechanical philosophers. Generally, these philosophers believed that they could explain most of the material world in terms of matter in motion and the impact of one body on another. They did not believe in causation at a distance; they regarded matter as passive and rejected active powers in matter. In England, Robert Boyle, the metaphysically minded chemist who led the scientific group that founded the Royal Society, classed both atomism and Cartesian matter as forms of corpuscularianism. He downplayed the differences between them. Both atomists and Cartesians believed that there were insensible particles that make up macro-sized bodies. But the atomists held that the particles were indivisible while the Cartesians did not, claiming that matter was infinitely divisible. It is noteworthy that Locke did not follow Boyle in his treatment of Descartes and the Cartesians; he is at pains to refute important aspects of the Cartesian account of body and mind.

'Plenum' means full. A plenum theory holds that the universe is full of matter and that there is consequently no void or empty space in the universe. Aristotle was a plenum theorist, as was Descartes. Descartes believed that there were three kinds of matter, all of different density. Each was made up of particles that could be infinitely divided and particles of different kinds could interpenetrate. It might seem that if the universe were full of matter then nothing could move, for there would be no empty space to move in. But this problem could be solved. Descartes had a vortex theory of motion: particles move circularly and they move together.

Pierre Gassendi had revived Epicurean atomism and made it safe for Christian intellectuals by purging it of the anti-theistic character that it had in antiquity. Instead of the world being eternal and uncreated, for example, Gassendi made the world finite and gave God the role of creating the world and putting the atoms into motion. Since God put the atoms into motion, no Epicurean swerve was required to explain the origin of the world.

Question

13. How do plenum theories of the universe differ from atomic theories?

Solidity and transdiction

Locke remarks of the idea of solidity: 'This of all other, seems the *Idea* most intimately connected with, and essential to Body ...' (II. IV. 1. 29–30.: 123). This makes it clear that solidity is the most important of the primary qualities of body. The Cartesian account of the essence of body is that it is flexible, movable and extended. So, it is also clear that Locke is emphatically rejecting the Cartesian account of the essence of material bodies. The opposite of solidity is void space. This was a topic about which there was considerable controversy in the seventeenth century. Atomists believed that solid atoms moved in void space. Others argued that the very notion of void space was incoherent: 'nature abhors a vacuum'. Old debates about void space centred in the seventeenth century around experiments using the recently invented vacuum or air pump. These pumps took all the air out of glass vessels. What was left inside? Robert Boyle and Thomas Hobbes argued about these matters.

What Locke is trying to do in chapter IV of Book II is to provide an empirical account of solidity. Solidity is related to impenetrability. 'The *Idea* of Solidity we receive by our Touch; and it arises from the resistance which we find in Body, to the entrance of any other Body into the Place it possesses, till it has left' (II. IV. 1. 27–1.: 122–3). Locke then proceeds to distinguish the idea of solidity from the mathematical idea of a solid figure, and from the ideas of space and hardness respectively. The idea of pure space is not compatible either with resistance or motion. Hardness consists 'in the firm Cohesion of the parts of Matter, making up masses of a sensible bulk, so that the whole does not easily change its Figure' (II. IV. 4. 3–5.: 125). Locke goes on to make the point that water possesses solidity as much as a diamond or adamant.

Locke then remarks that solidity allows us to distinguish the extension of body from the extension of space (see II. IV. 5. 9–13.: 126). Locke argues that the idea of pure space can be reached through thought experiments that do not beg the question of the vacuum. He claims that these ideas of pure space and solidity are clear and distinct. Note that at II. IV. 1. 19–26.: 123, Locke makes the claim that solidity is essential to body.

There is a significant tension between Locke's emphasis on experience as the source of all our ideas and the idea of atomism. Atoms are invisible. So how are we supposed to relate the atomic theory to experience? In the passage just cited above, we have an inference from the observation of macro-sized objects to unobserved micro-sized objects. Maurice Mandelbaum in his book *Philosophy, Science and Sense Perception* called this a transdictive inference. Mandelbaum writes that he took the term from Donald C. Williams. Williams heard Carl Hempel talk about the conditions under which one can use data to predict future events or explain past ones (that is make inductive inferences). Williams wanted to do something else with the data provided by experience. Mandelbaum continues: 'Professor Williams, however, wished to use data in such a way as so not only to be able to move back and forth *within* experience, but to be able to say something meaningful and true about what lay beyond the boundaries of possible experience. This he termed *transdiction*.' (Mandelbaum: 61). Mandelbaum claims that Locke's atomism, like that of Boyle and Newton, involves him in these kinds of transdictive inferences. The attribution of primary qualities to atoms seems to involve precisely this kind of inference.

If transdictive inferences are legitimate in Locke, this suggests that he is not what is sometimes called a meaning empiricist. A meaning empiricist, such as Berkeley in the eighteenth century or A.J. Ayer in the twentieth, holds that the meaning of terms is limited by experience. All claims about things that we cannot experience must be meaningless. It is for just this reason that Berkeley rejects the existence of atoms or matter as meaningless and incoherent, and Ayer rejects certain religious and metaphysical claims for similar reasons. Locke, by contrast, holds that we can meaningfully talk about things of which we have no experience (such as atoms) by analogy to things of which we do have experience. Still, the tension between Locke's empiricism and his atomism strongly colors Locke's views about what we can know about substances and the possibility of the study of nature becoming a science.

Questions

14. What relation does the question about the relation of solidity to body have to the debate between atomic and plenum theories of the universe?
15. What is a transdictive inference and how does it help us in categorizing Locke's brand of empiricism?

Primary, secondary and tertiary qualities

Book II chapter VIII introduces a distinction between the primary and secondary qualities of bodies. If Locke's account of solidity in chapter IV gave a hint that we were reaching deep water, this chapter plunges us into the depths. Here we are dealing with the relation between appearance and reality. The distinction is between the inherent and essential properties of matter (the primary qualities) and those that are relative to the perceiver (the secondary ones). The question is how to distinguish and yet connect appearance and reality. It turns out that this raises extraordinarily difficult problems that are central to the interpretation of *An Essay Concerning Human Understanding* and to much philosophy both before and after Locke.

The kind of realism that the distinction represents in Locke is the hallmark of Locke's brand of empiricism. This kind of empiricism holds that experience provides the building blocks from which knowledge is constructed, but does not entirely confine our knowledge to experience. In this, Locke is a very different kind of empiricist from Berkeley or Hume. In the case of primary and secondary qualities there is an even more striking point to notice: Locke is demonstrating that though it is rooted in experience, science can be used to correct some features of our ordinary experience.

The distinction between primary and secondary qualities has a long history, beginning with the Greek atomists and continuing with Galileo, Descartes and Boyle. Locke, it is generally supposed, took over the distinction from Boyle and popularized Boyle's terms for the distinction – primary, secondary and tertiary qualities. Boyle makes the distinction within a corpuscularian or atomic theory of matter in *The Origins of Forms and Qualities* (Boyle, Vol. III: 1–37). Locke's distinction is intended to serve two roles. Primary qualities are supposed to be objective features that resemble the ideas that they cause in us and to be physical features that a viable physical theory will use as the basis for explaining other phenomena.

Here again we find the question of how a theory of insensible particles can be squared with Locke's insistence on experience. Are we to understand the distinction as a theoretical one or one based in experience? Or can the two be combined? Locke's account of this important distinction has its difficulties and obscurities and these have given rise to much commentary, controversy and differing interpretations. Berkeley's First Dialogue in the *Three Dialogues between Hylas and Philonous* is almost entirely devoted to the refutation of the distinction (Berkeley, Vol. 2: 171–207). While Berkeley is an empiricist, he is also an idealist who rejects the existence of matter.

Our difficulties begin with deciding which qualities qualify as primary and which as secondary. Locke provides 26 lists of primary qualities in II. VIII. Robert Wilson, in 'Locke's Primary Qualities', claims that when one compares the lists one ends up with the following eight (or eleven?) qualities: 'bulk (or size), figure (or shape), solidity, extension, texture and situation, number and motion (or mobility)' (Wilson: 216). Not all commentators accept that all the qualities on this list are primary qualities. Peter Alexander, for example, holds that for Locke there are only three primary qualities: size, shape and mobility. According to Alexander, some of the other terms in Locke's list simply refer to these three qualities, i.e. bulk, extension, figure, motion and rest. Others, such as solidity, texture, situation, number and motion of parts are not primary qualities at all (Wilson: 201). Wilson explains that Alexander determines which of the qualities on Locke's lists are to count as primary qualities on the basis of an overarching corpuscularian interpretation. 'According to Alexander, primary qualities are qualities that the most fundamental things – single corpuscles – have in and of themselves, and that are to be invoked in providing non-occult explanations for the observable properties possessed by observable bodies' (Wilson: 201). It is because of this assumption that such properties as texture, number and motion of parts become problematic. In the view of seventeenth-century atomists, single atoms have neither parts nor textures; as texture strongly suggests an arrangement or organization of atoms. Scholarly differences over how many primary qualities there are shows that interpretation is already hard at work.

Turning to secondary or sensible qualities, we get colours, tastes, sounds, smells and some qualities derived from touch like heat and cold, but not solidity. Additionally the primary qualities have powers to affect other things, just as the sun has the power to melt wax. These are the tertiary powers. The list of secondary qualities seems to be significantly less controversial than the list of primary qualities. Still, there is one major question about secondary qualities: do they exist in the object or only in the mind? Another way of putting this is that there is a clear distinction between primary qualities and the ideas of primary qualities; one causes the other. Is there a similar clear distinction between secondary qualities and ideas of secondary qualities, or are secondary qualities just ideas of secondary qualities?

Locke says that secondary qualities are: 'nothing in the Objects themselves, but Powers to produce various Sensations in us by their *primary qualities*, i.e. by the bulk, figure, texture and motions of their insensible parts' (II. VIII. 10. 17–19.: 135). An influential interpretation of this passage deriving from Berkeley takes the first clause to assert that secondary qualities are not in the objects themselves. In that case, they must only be in the mind and be identical with the ideas of secondary qualities. But it is a mistake to read this passage in this way. Locke tells us that secondary qualities are powers in the object to produce various sensations in us. Thus, there is as clear a distinction between secondary qualities and ideas of secondary qualities as there is between primary qualities and ideas of primary qualities. It is just that secondary qualities are a certain set of primary qualities or combinations of them that have certain effects on us and these effects do not resemble their causes.

Locke claims that the primary qualities exist in bodies whether we perceive them or not. Secondary qualities, on the other hand, are simply powers of the primary qualities to produce particular effects in us. Primary qualities like solidity, extension or motion do not require perceivers to be complete, while secondary qualities do. When a tree falls in the forest with no one around to hear it there exist all the conditions for the falling to be heard except for some sentient being actually to hear it. Locke seems to hold that this difference is crucial. We assume that the tree can fall without us being there; the question is whether there can be a sound without someone to hear it. Clearly what is meant here is a heard or sensible sound, not simply sound waves emanating from a source. Clearly, you need a hearer in order to have a heard sound, so without the hearer the relationship is incomplete. It is the difference between an essential or inherent quality and a relational one that is neither essential nor inherent, though one terminus of that relation is in the object. This emphasis on experienced qualities connects with Locke's empiricism. One can talk to a blind person about light waves and wavelengths and explain where scarlet is on the spectrum, but that does not help a blind person to have the experience of scarlet.

In sections 11 through 13 Locke considers how qualities of both kinds are caused in us. He claims that bodies produce ideas in us by impulse (see II. VIII.12.: 136). The passing remark that if external objects 'be not united to our Minds, when they produce *Ideas* in it' is about the only reference I can detect in the entire chapter to the scholastic doctrine of intelligible or intentional species. Locke seems simply to be dismissing it in favour of the doctrines of mechanical philosophy. He goes on in section 12 to argue that secondary qualities are caused in us in the same way that primary qualities are, even though 'God should annex such *Ideas* to such Motions, with which they have no similitude; than that he should annex the *Idea* of Pain to the notion of a piece of Steel dividing our Flesh, with which that *Idea* hath no resemblance' (II. VIII. 13. 30–2.: 136–7). The ideas that bodies only affect other bodies, including our own, by impulse and the idea that both primary and secondary qualities are caused in the same way plays a significant role in Locke's arguments for making the distinction.

In sections 16 through 20 of chapter VIII Locke gives a series of arguments on behalf of the distinction. It is often contended that the arguments that Locke gives are a mixed bag, some good, some bad and some indifferent. (Mackie: 20–5). There is little doubt that this is true. Yet there are some important points that Locke makes along the way that are worth noting. Locke begins by asking the man who thinks heat is in the fire 'what Reason he has to say, That his *Idea of Warmth* which was produced by the Fire, is actually *in the Fire*; and his *Idea of Pain*, which the same Fire produced in him the same way, is *not* in the Fire' (II. VIII. 16. 27–32.: 137). Locke thinks that upon reflection such a man will see that neither the warmth nor the pain are in the fire. Both are caused by the bulk, figure and motion of the parts, which these effects do not resemble. In section 18 he makes a similar point about whiteness and sweetness, but now we also get ideas of primary qualities. A particular piece of manna may be round or square and in motion. 'This *Idea* of Motion represents it, as it really is in the *Manna* moving: A Circle or Square are the same, whether in *Idea* or Existence; in the Mind or in the *Manna*: And this, both *Motion and Figure really are in the Manna*, whether we take notice of them or no: This every Body is willing to agree to' (II. VIII. 18. 10–15.: 138). The next thing that everyone will agree to is that the bulk, figure and texture of the manna can cause sensations of sickness and pain within us and that these sensations are not in the manna and do not exist when they are not felt by us (see II. VIII. 18. 31–2.: 138–9). These ideas are caused by the operation of the manna in us. And so are the ideas of the whiteness and sweetness of the manna. But Locke says that: 'Men are hardly brought to think, that Sweetness and Whiteness are not in the Manna ...' (II. VIII. 18. 20–21: 138). Locke is arguing that given the premises that the ordinary person accepts, to hold that secondary qualities are in the object or that sensations such as pain are not, involves them in a paradox that requires explanation. The corpuscularian alternative does not have this problem.

In section 19 Locke argues from an example of a piece of porphyry that there is a power in the rock to produce the different colours we see, but that no real alterations are made in the porphyry when its colours change and that it continues to exist in the absence of seen colour. In section 20 he gives the example of pounding an almond in a pestle, to make the point that it is by changing the texture of the almond in this mechanical way that the colour and taste are altered.

Finally, in section 21, he argues that the corpuscularian hypothesis explains in a perfectly clear way why the same water at the same time feels warm to one hand but cold to the other. This last example may well have two targets. The first is the position of the ordinary man whom Locke has been addressing from section 16 on. But this is a more puzzling case, and the apparent contradiction of the water being both warm and cold suggests that Locke may have been trying to resolve a sceptical problem about perception on the basis of the corpuscular hypothesis. Locke's treatment of this case is strikingly different from that of Berkeley in the first of the *Three Dialogues between Hylas and Philonous.* Berkeley, in contrast with Locke, is using the apparent contradiction to argue that secondary qualities are only in the mind. Berkeley may have believed that this was also Locke's view. If so, he was surely mistaken.

Questions

16. What are the primary qualities? Are there primary qualities of atoms and primary qualities of macro-sized objects? How are these similar to and different from one another?
17. Are there ideas of primary qualities that are sensible in the way that colour is sensible?
18. On Locke's account are there secondary qualities or only ideas of secondary qualities?

Resemblance and representative theories of perception

Locke claims that the ideas of primary qualities resemble the qualities in the objects while ideas of secondary qualities do not (see II. VIII. 7. 7–16.: 134). Scholars have puzzled over what 'resemblance' means here. Mandelbaum, for example, in explaining why Locke's atomism may have received so little attention up to that point, notes that:

> In his well known distinction between primary and secondary qualities Locke states that 'the ideas of primary qualities of bodies are resemblances of them, and their patterns do really exist in the bodies themselves.' Yet no atomist can consistently

hold that the specific qualities that we perceive when we look at or when we touch material objects are identical with the qualities which these objects, when considered as congeries of atoms, actually do possess. For example, the continuous contour which characterizes the perceived shape of an object such as a table cannot be considered by an atomist to be a wholly adequate representation of that object's true shape. (Mandelbaum: 15)

We can note that Locke claims it is a mistake to think that our perceptions 'are exactly the Images and *Resemblances* of something inherent in the subject'. So there may well be some question not only as to which ideas resemble qualities, but the degree to which they resemble them. Locke might hold, for example, that the ideas of primary qualities resemble their causes, because they share the same kind of quality, e.g. shape, but not the same exact shape. In the technical language of contemporary philosophy, they share the same determinable but not the same determinate shape. This is, in effect, Mandelbaum's interpretation. He thinks that Locke would hold that ideas of secondary qualities and their causes do not share a determinable (Mandelbaum: 21–2). So the idea of a motion of a body and the actual motion of that body share the determinable motion while the idea of red and the cause of that idea do not share a determinable.

It is also worth considering whether, when Locke tells us that it is usual to think that all of our ideas are images and resemblances of the qualities in an object, he is concerned with the way people ordinarily think or if he is making reference to the scholastic/ Aristotelian theory taught in the universities at that time. If the former, the justification for the claim of resemblance would be that the ideas seem to be in the object, e.g. the apple appears green. On the scholastic theory, however, there is a claim that the *intelligible or intentional species* of the object is transmitted to us. As a consequence of this, all our ideas resemble the qualities in the objects they come from. But on either a pre-theoretical or scholastic theory of perception, colour and heat are as much in the object as are extension and motion. So on either the ordinary person's conception or the scholastic one, our ideas of colours represent properties of an object as accurately as do our ideas of extension and motion (see II. VIII. 16. 18–23.: 137). This is the idea that Locke believes is shown to be false by the distinction between primary and secondary qualities. Some scholars have claimed that it is the scholastic doctrine that Locke is aiming at, and yet he never mentions it explicitly, while he does talk about our ordinary experience in this respect. Even if Locke has the scholastic doctrine of intelligible or intentional species in mind, it is not clear how simply offering an alternative corpuscularian account solves the problem of resemblance.

In *Problems from Locke*, J.L. Mackie remarks that there is a major difficulty for Locke's distinction between primary and secondary qualities.

> It is formulated within the framework of a representative theory of perception which distinguishes sharply between ideas in our minds, and any externally real things, while postulating that our ideas are causally produced by those external things acting upon our sense organs and through them our brains, and yet assumes that we can speak intelligibly about some of our ideas and those external realities. (Mackie: 27–8)

What is a representative theory of perception and why would it be a problem for Locke if he held such a theory? Representative theories of perception are typically triadic relationships between perceivers, ideas or sense data, and physical objects. On such a theory what I immediately see are sense data or ideas that are caused by objects and these ideas in turn represent those objects. So what immediately appear to me are ideas, and the material objects that can cause ideas, while only encountered mediately, are still real. Realist theories of perception, on the other hand, tend to claim that the relation between perceiver and the thing perceived is a dyadic relation. I see the apple directly; there is no intermediary idea or sense data.

Representational theories give us the problem of resemblance in a very general form. Locke claims that ideas of primary qualities resemble the qualities in the object, while ideas of secondary qualities do not. But if all we perceive immediately are ideas, how do we know that the ideas accurately or inaccurately represent the things that cause them? We would need to perceive the objects themselves to compare them with our ideas. But we only experience ideas and not objects. This view of the implications of representative theories of perception has been called the veil of perception or sometimes the picture/original theory doctrine. Montaigne put the point nicely a hundred years before Locke. He writes in *An Apology for Raymond Sebond*: 'And as for saying that the impressions of the senses convey to the soul the quality of foreign objects by resemblance, how can the soul make sure of this resemblance, having of itself no communication with foreign objects? Just as a man who does not know Socrates, seeing his portrait, cannot say that it resembles him' (Montaigne: 186).

A crucial feature of the problem is that it is global. All our ideas exist on the side of appearance while all the material objects that cause our ideas are on the side of reality. The dilemma is that on the one hand the distinction between primary and secondary qualities seems to require a representational theory of perception, but the nature of such representational theories is such that they do not provide any basis for making the distinction. Because of the global nature of the problem, it has significant commonalities with the problems posed by Descartes' Dream and Evil Demon hypotheses in the *Meditations*. Descartes' solution is to invoke a range of innate ideas and then use these to connect reality with appearance. This solution is not open to Locke.

We might also note that Locke himself seems to be perfectly aware of the picture/original analogy and the problem associated with it. In his *An Examination of the Opinions of P. Malebranche in seeing all Things in God*, Locke remarks: 'In his Eclaircissements on the Nature of Ideas, pg. 535 of the quarto edition, he says that "he is certain that the ideas of things are unchangeable." This I cannot comprehend; for how can I know that the picture of any thing is like that thing, when I never see that which it represents?' (Locke, 1823, Vol. IX: 250).

Some scholars such as A.O. Woozley and John Yolton have concluded that because Locke was aware of the problem raised by the picture/original conception of perception, that he must not have held a representational theory of perception. J.L. Mackie, however, notes that the view that Malebranche holds is significantly different from that of Locke. The idea that Locke is criticizing involves representation without the things represented playing any causal role in the production of their representation.

Mackie, however, thinks that Locke concedes that the picture/original analogy applies to his own theory, but thinks he can solve the problem it poses (see Mackie: 38–9). In Book IV, when he is discussing real knowledge, Locke raises the puzzle (see IV. IV. 3.

27–34.: 563). In this passage the two kinds of real ideas Locke mentions are simple ideas and modes. In considering the distinction between primary and secondary qualities, we are concerned with simple ideas and not with modes. The examples that Locke gives of actual simple ideas are both ideas of secondary qualities, whiteness and brightness. This suggests that simple ideas of both primary and secondary qualities are real. Locke explains what he means by real ideas. Ideas are real if they have 'a Foundation in Nature, such as have a Conformity with the real Being, and Existence, of Things or their Archetypes' (II. XXX. 1. 11–17.: 372). He goes on to say explicitly that in this sense all simple ideas are real, 'all agree to the reality of things' (II. XXX. 2. 19–20.: 372). Thus both primary and secondary qualities are real (see II. XXX. 2. 20–6.: 372–3). So, on Locke's view, as long as the effects have a steady correspondence to their causes in things outside us, whether they resemble the qualities in the object or not, they are real.

If we recall the point that Mackie makes about the importance of causality to Locke's resemblance thesis, Locke would hold that Malebranche could not account for ideas being real in this sense, because there is no causal connection between objects and ideas in his theory. In fact, in the continuation of the passage quoted earlier, Locke says that the only other possible meaning he can give to Malebranche's remark is the tautology that an idea will always be the same as itself and: 'Thus the idea of a horse, and the idea of a centaur, will, as often as they recur in my mind, be unchangeably the same; which is no more than this; the same idea will always be the same idea; but whether the one or the other be the true representation of any thing that exists, that, upon his principles, neither our author nor any body else can know' (Locke, 1823, Vol. IX: 250). Hence, without the causal connection between things and ideas, Malebranche would have no basis to argue that our ideas of horses conform to things while our ideas of centaurs do not. Locke holds that his own account, with its crucial causal component, fares better. Locke takes up these issues again in Book IV. We will return to them at that point.

Locke's account of primary and secondary qualities leads naturally to a discussion of substance. This takes us from chapter VIII of Book II to chapter XXIII, 'Of Our Complex Ideas of Substance'.

Questions

19. What does Locke mean when he says that ideas of primary qualities resemble their causes while the ideas of secondary qualities do not?
20. What does Locke mean when he says that the primary qualities are real?
21. When Locke says that secondary qualities are real is he using a different sense of the term 'real' from the one he uses when he says primary qualities are real? If so, what is the difference?
22. What is a representative theory of perception? Why does the distinction between primary and secondary qualities require a representative or causal theory of perception?
23. What problem does adopting a representative theory of perception pose for the distinction between primary and secondary qualities?

Space, solidity, the vacuum and substance

In chapter XIII Locke turns to our ideas of space. There was a significant debate over the nature of space that went back to Aristotle and the atomists of antiquity. The atomists affirmed, and Aristotle denied, that it was possible to have a perfect vacuum in space. This debate continued through the Middle Ages and into the seventeenth century with the reemergence of atomism as a serious intellectual doctrine.

Locke takes the idea of space to be a simple idea. He claims that he has shown previously 'that we get the idea of space by our Sight and Touch,' that is by seeing the distance between bodies or parts of bodies (II. XIII. 2. 11.: 167). He goes on to define a variety of terms including distance and capacity. He remarks that: 'Each different distance is a different Modification of Space, and *each* Idea *of any different distance, or Space*, is a simple Mode of this *Idea*' (II. XIII. 4. 21–23.: 167). The mind can create different measures of distance, such as inches, feet, fathoms, miles. These ideas are all made up of the idea of space. Men can repeat these measurements in their minds to get ideas such as long, square or cubic, and by joining them one to another to 'enlarge their Idea of Space as much as they please' (II. XIII. 4. 6.: 168). We thus get the idea of immensity. He next defines 'figure' and claims that the mind has an ability to make angles of any size and enclose spaces so as to make figures and shapes of infinite variety. He then turns to 'place' in sections 7–10 arguing that it is a position relative to other things and notes that this explains why we have no idea of what the place of the universe is.

In sections 11–16 in chapter XIII Locke offers his arguments against the Cartesian identification of body with extension. He also gives the argument for the vacuum, which he refers to in his discussion of solidity in chapter IV. We will begin with this even though it occurs later in the chapter since it looks back to chapter IV, while the discussion of extension and solidity leads into a discussion of substance which looks forward to chapter XXIII, 'Of Our Complex Ideas of Substances.'

Body, solidity and extension

Locke begins his attack on the identification of body with extension by claiming that the Cartesians are either changing the meaning of the word 'body' or else are confusing two very different ideas with one another. He doesn't think they would change the meaning of the word because they complain about other people doing this. On the other hand what most people mean by 'body' is 'something that is solid and extended, whose parts are separable and movable in different ways; and what most people mean by 'extension' is 'only the Space that lies between the Extremities of those solid coherent Parts, and which is possessed by them' (II. XIII. 11. 30–34.: 171). So, the Cartesians can choose which of these two unpleasant alternatives they are willing to accept. Or because Locke says they would not do the first, he is suggesting that they really are confusing two quite distinct ideas one with the other.

Locke goes on to point out that something being extended is a necessary condition for it being solid, but they are still completely distinct ideas. He continues: 'Solidity is so inseparable an Idea from Body, that upon that depends its filling of Space, its Contact, its Impulse, and Communication of Motion upon Impulse' (II. XIII. 11. 9–11.: 172). He makes the argument that if the Cartesians hold that mind and body are distinct because 'thinking includes not the *Idea* of Extension in it; the same reason will be as valid, I suppose, to prove that *Space is not Body*, because it includes not the *Idea* of Solidity in it' (II. XIII. 11. 13–15.: 172). He then makes the point that body and extension are different, because the parts of space are inseparable, immovable and without resistance to the motion of body (II. XIII. 14. 13–15.: 173).

This first section of the argument is perhaps the most important, because Locke is trying to make the Cartesians accept atomist premises by arguing that solidity and extension are different from one another. Descartes would take this distinction between extension and solidity as a plausible mistake and would not accept these Lockean arguments or their conclusions.

Locke expects that the Cartesians will raise some objections. First, there is the dilemma that either space is something or nothing. If space is nothing, then there is nothing between two bodies and they must necessarily be touching. If space is something, the Cartesians will ask if it is a body or a spirit? Locke's reply is to ask a rhetorical question: 'Who told them that there was, or could be nothing, but solid Beings, which could not think; and thinking Beings that were not extended' (II. XIII. 16. 32–34.: 173). The point clearly implied by this rhetorical question is that body and spirit as defined do not exhaust the possibilities. In addition to solid objects there is empty space.

No clear and distinct idea of substance

The next question Locke thinks he will be asked is whether this space void of bodies is a substance or an accident. He says that he does not know and 'nor shall I be ashamed to own my Ignorance, till they that ask, shew me a clear distinct Idea of Substance' (II. XIII. 17. 2–4.: 174).

Locke spends sections 18–20 arguing that we do not have a clear and distinct idea of substance. This is worth noting because the passage was taken by one of Locke's critics, Bishop Stillingfleet, to mean that Locke thought there was no such thing as substance. But Locke's point is not that we do not have an idea of substance; it is simply that we do not have a clear and distinct one. Rather, our idea of substance is obscure, confused and relative. And, since it is not clear and distinct, Locke has a good reason for not knowing whether empty space is a substance or not (see II. XIII. 18. 5–11.: 174).

Locke then proceeds to note that those who put so much emphasis on the word 'substance', presumably the Cartesians, if they apply it to such utterly distinct things as God, spirits and bodies in the same way, then God, spirits and bodies 'differ not any otherwise than in a bare different modification of that *Substance*; as a Tree and a Pebble, being in the same sense Body, and agreeing in the common nature of Body, differ only in a bare modification of that common matter; which will be a very harsh doctrine' (II. XIII. 18. 17–22.: 174). It is difficult to figure out exactly what Locke has in mind here. But the point seems to be that God must be so different from spirits and bodies that one would really not want to say that they have as much in common as the analogy with the tree and the pebble would imply, and yet this seems to be the implication of each of them being a substance. The alternative is that they are so different that substance is being used in three different senses. But if this is so, then it would seem appropriate to make clear what these distinct senses of the word are and perhaps use three different words for them. And if there are three such distinct meanings, Locke says, why not add a fourth one that would allow empty space to be a substance in a different sense from the other three?

Why Locke thinks that the first part of the dilemma he is posing works is a little puzzling. If the term 'substance' represents a very high level of abstraction, in which particular differences have been systematically removed and all that is left is a very general term, then it would seem that very different things could be called 'substances' without in any way suggesting that they are alike, or generating that 'very harsh doctrine'. But setting aside this worry for the moment, let us see what else Locke has to say.

In section 19 Locke takes up a new line of argument (see II. XIII. 19. 1–14.: 175). Locke is arguing that the distinction between substances and the accidents they support is not helpful. This also seems to be an example of the theme announced at the beginning of section 18, that making up names for things we don't understand only lets us feign knowledge where we have none. But the last sentence makes it clear that we do have an idea of substance, 'but it is only an obscure one of what it does'.

In section 20 Locke continues the argument begun in the previous section that 'the Doctrine of *Substance* and *Accidents*' has very little use in philosophy. He gives examples of two analogous explanations that are clearly inadequate. The first is of an American Indian having the functions of a pillar and its base explained to him as the base supporting the pillar and the pillar being supported by the base. Locke says: 'Would he not think himself mocked instead of taught, with such an account as this?' (II. XIII. 20. 19–21.: 175). The other example is of a stranger to books who is told that: 'all learned books consisted of Paper and Letters, and that Letters were things inhering in Paper, and Paper a thing that held forth Letters; a notable way of having clear *Ideas* of Letters and Paper' (II. XIII. 20. 23–26.: 175). Locke claims that our ideas of substance and accident are defined in an equally circular and uninformative way. Thus, they will be of little use in helping us to decide whether empty space is a substance or an accident.

Questions

24. What are Locke's reasons for holding that solidity is part of our idea of body?
25. How does Locke's disagreement with the Cartesians about space involve the notion of substance?
26. What problems does Locke have with the idea of substance?

Infinite space and the vacuum

Locke continues the argument against the Cartesians in sections 21 through 23 by posing several thought experiments. The first goes to prove, against the Cartesians, that space is infinite. Descartes had been unwilling to say this, allowing only that space was indeterminate. Locke imagines a man placed by God at the point where the last body in the universe exists. The man stretches out his arm and either finds some hindrance to his extending his arm or does not. If nothing hinders, then it is plain that space extends out past the last body. If something does hinder the man's arm, Locke wants the Cartesians to tell him whether what hinders the arm in this case is substance or accident. He thinks when they have answered this question they can then determine what it is that is between two bodies at some distance from one another.

The second involves the supposition that God could bring all motion in the universe to a complete halt and then destroy a piece of matter. What would be left when that piece had been destroyed would be a vacuum, for *ex hypothesi*, nothing could move into the space where the body had been before it was destroyed. To deny that this could be done would be to impugn God's omnipotence.

Locke gives a third argument from the motion of bodies. In effect, he claims that empty space is required to move the parts of bodies freely within their boundaries. This is yet another transdictive argument arising from the way in which matter in motion works in medium sized bodies to how it must work in minute ones.

The point is that empty space is required for motion at whatever scale.

Locke adds two more arguments in sections 23 and 24. The first of these begins with the claim that since the issue is about the idea of space or extension being the same as the idea of body, no proof is required of the real existence of the vacuum. All that is required is a proof that the idea of a vacuum exists. And Locke thinks it is plain that those who dispute the existence of a vacuum have such an idea when they dispute whether it exists or not. For, he says, 'if they had not the *Idea* of Space without Body, they could not make a question about its existence' (II. XIII. 23. 13–14.: 178). And, on the other hand, if they had no idea of body that did not include something more than the bare idea of space, they could not imagine anything other than the plenitude of the world. So, our ability to have these disputes shows that we at least have the ideas of solid bodies and empty space.

Question

27. What are we to make of the argument that we don't need proof that the vacuum exists, only proof that the idea of a vacuum exists? If people were disputing about the existence of unicorns, would it really make a strong point to demonstrate that both disputants had the same idea of what a unicorn is? If this analogy is not compelling, what is the difference between the two cases?

In sections 24 and 25 Locke reflects on how the Cartesian came to make the mistake of confounding two quite different ideas that he attributed to them back in section 11. He notes that the idea of extension 'joins itself so inseparably with all visible and most tangible Qualities, that it suffers us to see no one, or feel very few external Objects, without taking in impressions of Extension too' (II. XIII. 24. 21–24.: 178). Locke thinks that not seeing any bodies that were without extension, the Cartesians concluded that this was the essence of bodies. (This is a pretty implausible account of why Descartes came to this conclusion). Locke suggests that if they had considered ideas of tastes and smells and hunger and thirst, they would have found bodily ideas that do not have the idea of extension included in them. Finally, he notes in section 25 that unity too is an idea that goes with every body, but it will hardly do to say that unity is the essence of every body.

Material objects and substance

Our ideas about substances comprise one of the major categories of complex ideas. 'Substance' is a term that shows up almost as frequently as the word 'idea' in the *Essay*. One common way of thinking about substance is that it represents something independently existing as opposed to qualities that cannot exist independently. At least one scholar has suggested that Locke does not have this conception of substance in mind, but that surely is not true. Still, understanding Locke's account of substance is difficult for a number of reasons. Locke uses different terms, 'substratum', 'substance in general', 'essence', 'real essence' and 'nominal essence' in his extended discussion of 'substance' in the course of the *Essay*. There has been considerable scholarly debate about how these various terms relate to one another in Locke's own account of substance and to the views of the scholastics, the corpuscularians and ordinary people. There are various possible positions. Let us, then, turn to Book II, chapter XXIII.

Locke begins the chapter by explaining how we come by our ideas of substance and some of the mistakes we make along the way (see II. XXIII. 1. 4–16.: 295). Locke is telling us that our ideas of substances arise because we notice that many of our simple ideas go together. Locke would have done better to say that we notice that many qualities go together, for it is clear that when he says 'which being presumed to belong to one thing' he means qualities in the object and not ideas in the mind. Thus, if we were to take the passage before the introduction of the term 'substratum', it might suggest that a substance is just a clump of qualities that we notice go constantly together. But Locke thinks that we go beyond this to suggest something that holds all those qualities together, which he calls 'substratum' and 'substance'. If this is an account of what ordinary people think, Locke is probably wrong about this. What seems more likely is that only a few philosophers have this idea of substance.

Locke believes that there are several mistakes we regularly make in respect of substances. To begin with, we may fail to remember that our idea of a substance is a collection of simple ideas and treat it as if it were one simple idea. Here again Locke should probably have written 'quality' and not 'idea'. We make the mistake of thinking that a substance is one quality, because we think there is one thing wherein the qualities subsist 'and from which they do result'. The term 'substratum' here seems to be identified with that in which qualities inhere and from which they result, and is equivalent to the term 'substance'.

In the next section Locke addresses the idea of 'pure substance in general' (see II. XXII. 2. 17–6.: 295–6). So, the qualities that produce simple ideas in us are commonly called 'accidents'. The supposition of an unknown support for qualities is ambiguous. Such a support could be knowable but not known, or it could be unknowable in principle. The former sort of support might be the congeries of primary qualities that the ideas of primary and secondary qualities result from. But Locke seems to be clearly implying that there is a deeper level by asking, 'what it is that Solidity and Extension inheres in'.

There is an old argument suggesting that just as there are clear differences between subjects and predicates in language, so there is a difference between substances and qualities in the world. Qualities cannot exist independently. But what is it that they inhere in? It must be, goes the argument, something without qualities. But such a pure logical subject being without any qualities must be quite unknowable in principle. It is regularly suggested that Locke accepts this argument. Over the last 40 years, such notable scholars as Peter Alexander, Maurice Mandelbaum and Michael Ayers have disputed this claim. Ayers argues that Locke's position on substance derives from Gassendi and that, in effect, he holds that the real essences of things and not a bare particular or logical subject is what Locke has in mind (Ayers, Vol. II: 28–9). The real essences of things are in their atomic constitution and so are in principle knowable, though Locke thinks we do not and probably will never come to know them (see II. XXIII. 3. 20–25.: 296).

Locke is critical of those who use Latin terms to conceal their ignorance. But, on the other hand, it would seem that if the substratum is a logical subject with no qualities, then we should simply note its unknowable character and chide those who have pretensions of knowing what cannot be known. But something seems to be wrong here. At the beginning of his discussion of substance in general, Locke asks what the secondary qualities of colour or weight inhere in, and answers that it is the solid extended parts. He then asks what solidity and extension inhere in. Locke then compares our inability to answer the last question to the Indian who, believing that he had to explain what supports the earth, answered that the earth rests on a great tortoise, and when asked what the tortoise rests on, answers that it rests on 'I know not what' (II. XXIII. 2. 21–6.: 295–6). The similarity in structure between Locke's questions about what secondary and primary qualities inhere in and the questions about what support the earth are hard to miss. The comparison, while famous, may not be well conceived. If Locke believes that this regress of questions really does terminate in a logical subject that has no qualities, is in principle unknowable and which is reached by a process of abstraction; why compare it to a case where the attempt to give an explanation is ill conceived from the start and where the answer 'I know not what' is the indication of the failure of the explanation and where no process of abstraction is involved? Locke goes on sarcastically to compare European scholastic philosophers, who came up with the doctrine of substance and accidents, to the Indian and suggests that they pretend to know what they do not know, and pretend to have an explanation of what accidents inhere in when they do not. But the Indian knows that he doesn't know what the tortoise rests on. At the least, these dissimilarities are likely to cause confusion, and led Leibniz in the *New Essays Concerning Human Understanding* to claim that it was Locke who is confused (Leibniz: 219.) Locke may well have been trying to do too much with this comparison.

In his discussion of the comparison with the Indian in the *New Essays* Leibniz notes that to demand that a pure logical subject without qualities should explain what qualities one thing has rather than another is to ask the impossible (Leibniz: 219). But Locke doesn't seem to be making this mistake. At the beginning of II. XXIII. 3 he remarks that the ideas of particular sorts of substances are made by 'collecting such Combinations of simple *Ideas,* as are by Experience . . . taken notice of to exist together . . .' (II. XXIII. 3. 22–24.: 296). He goes on to say that these ideas are derived from the unknown essence of these things, presumably their atomic constitutions. These 'real essences' as he comes to call them in Book III are also unknown. But they are unknown for quite different reasons than substance in general. So, it is not substance in general that is supposed to explain why a particular thing has the qualities it has, but its atomic constitution. In the seventeenth century scientists could claim to know none of these real essences; Locke is at pains to make this point in Book III. But now physicists, chemists and biochemists know many real essences. So, in this case, our ignorance was contingent. Locke clearly thought that we would never know these real essences, but not for the same reason that it is not possible to know a quality-less logical subject.

Edwin McCann in 'Locke's Philosophy of Body' offers an appealing solution. Focusing on the passages in II. XXIII which seem to support the bare particulars account, McCann writes:

> If we read these passages carefully, we find Locke saying only that our idea of substance has nothing more in it than that it supports qualities. It does not follow from this that whatever answers to the idea of substance (if anything does) can have no other properties or features than that it supports qualities, which is what the bare-particulars doctrine requires. So, there is no need to attribute the bare-particulars doctrine to Locke. (McCann: 83)

While attractive, this solution seems a bit dubious, and for the same kinds of reasons that the real essence solution is dubious. When Locke goes through the secondary qualities and asks what they depend on, and then takes the answer, the primary qualities, and asks on what they depend, we are involved in a regress with no more plausible candidates. Ayers' answer is that it is only the extension and solidity of macro-sized objects that Locke is talking about in this passage. But if this were so, as J.L. Mackie remarks, it is a pity that Locke did not say so. It seems fairly clear that modern physics would stop the regress that leads to the 'I know not what' by appealing to such space occupying qualities as electric charge and resting mass. These qualities in turn would explain solidity and the other primary qualities. But Locke does not suggest that there is anything that will stop the regress in a satisfactory way. This is a problem equally for the Mandelbaum/Ayers thesis and for the McCann thesis. J.L. Mackie in *Problems from Locke* points to passages from the Locke-Stillingfleet correspondence that strongly suggest that Locke did accept the linguistic argument for a logical subject (Mackie: 78–82). But as Mackie points out, the argument is not a good one. Locke should have adopted either the solution proposed by Mandelbaum and Ayers or the one proposed by McCann.

Questions

28. What does the term 'substratum' add to the conception of substance as properties that clump together?
29. How does the real essence conception of substance (the Mandelbaum/Ayers thesis) differ from the logical subject conception?

Space, time, number and infinity

In chapters XIII through XVII Locke deals with issues closely related to the nature of physical bodies. Space, time, number and infinity are all, Locke claims, ideas that the mind makes from simple ideas derived from sensation. In each case, once we have the simple idea, we can make simple modes by the repetition of the same unit. So we get the idea of space by sight and touch and in particular by considering 'a distance between Bodies of different Colours or between the parts of the same Body ...' (II. XIII. 2. 13–14.: 167). Each different distance is a different modification of space and each different corresponding idea is a different simple mode of the idea. We have already considered much of the content of chapter XIII earlier so let us turn to time.

Locke notes that the ideas of time and eternity have been considered abstruse and puzzling, but proposes to apply the same kind of procedure to it that he applied to space, claiming that: 'I doubt not that but one of these Sources of all our Knowledge, *viz. Sensation and Reflection*, will be able to furnish us with these *Ideas*, as clear and distinct as many other, which are thought less obscure ...' (II. XIV. 2. 21–24.: 181). He traces the idea of succession to the train of ideas that constantly succeed one another in an alert mind. Reflection on this succession of ideas gives us the notion of succession and the distance between any two parts of that succession gives us the idea of duration. Locke distinguishes between succession of ideas and motion and argues that it is the succession of ideas and not motion that gives us our idea of duration. Once we have the idea of duration, as with space, we can measure the distance between parts, giving us our idea of time (II. XIV. 17.: 187). It is true that Locke thinks there is a disanalogy between space and time. Space and time differ in that the parts of space exist at the same time while the parts of time do not, but it turns out that this does not particularly hinder the measurement of duration. And just as we can extend our idea of space infinitely, we can do the same with duration to get the idea of eternity.

Up to this point we have not examined the chapters in Book II that deal with mixed modes and relations. Relations we will put off until the section of this chapter on 'Relations and moral relations', and the treatment of mixed modes will come in the course of dealing with Book III. We turn next to Locke's account of power, volition and freedom, personal identity and morality.

Power, volition and freedom

In the next two sections of this book we will examine Locke's account of volition, personal identity and morality. These chapters of the *Essay* fit together to form a view of persons and how they direct their lives towards happiness. This view underpins Locke's account of a rational religion in Book IV of the *Essay* and these chapters are quite interesting in and of themselves.

Chapter XXI 'Power', the longest chapter in the *Essay*, is important for several reasons. First, it takes us from the inherent properties of physical objects and space and time to a discussion of causality, or how physical objects affect one another. Analogously, it takes us in respect of minds from the reception and construction of ideas to volition and action. It is in this context that we get Locke's discussion of free will and determinism and our evaluation of acts as good and evil.

It is worth noting that the debate about free will and determinism occurred during this period both in the theological and the scientific domains. Free will was a Catholic doctrine. Luther and Calvin, the Protestant reformers, rejected free will in favour of divine determinism and predestination. If one considers omnipotence to be one of God's properties, it is easy to see how complete determinism of the created world might follow from this. Thomas Hobbes was both a theological and a scientific determinist. The Anglican Church, which was supposed to be a Protestant church, abandoned Lutheran and Calvinist determinism in favour of free will a decade or so before the publication (without the author's permission) of Hobbes's exchange with Bishop Bramhall in 1654. One of the points that Hobbes makes in defence of his position is that the leaders of the Protestants, Luther and Calvin, were determinists. Bramhall's rejection of this claim is quite implausible. Hobbes is also remarkable in drawing the determinist implications from the work of Galileo. (For a detailed account of Hobbes's determinism see Jürgen Oberhoff's fine book *Hobbes's Theory of the Will*). The point to be taken from all this is that while Locke, as it turns out, is a determinist, one should not assume that this makes him a scientific determinist opposing the religious doctrine of free will. Gideon Yaffe in *Liberty Worth the Name*, his fine study of Locke's account of free agency, claims that Locke does in fact subscribe to a form of theological determinism (Yaffe, 6–8).

Powers, active and passive

Locke begins by explaining how he thinks we come by the idea of *power* (see II. XXI. 1. 10–22.: 233). This passage suggests a number of things. First, we observe order in change. On many occasions we observe fire melting gold. We conclude that the same will happen in the future. This amounts to what we would call inductive reasoning: we expect that the future will resemble the past in relevant ways. We are also attributing to fire the causal power of melting gold and to gold the power to be melted. This suggests that there are both active and passive powers in matter. Locke, however, thinks that on closer examination we may conclude that while God has all active powers, matter has only passive powers. To find both together it is best to look at created spirits. We get the clearest idea of active powers from our own minds. Locke writes: 'The *Idea* of the beginning of motion, we have only from reflection on what passes in our selves, where we find by Experience, that barely by willing it, barely by a thought of the Mind, we can move the parts of our Bodies, which were before at rest' (II. XXI. 4. 30–33.: 235).

Locke now offers a series of definitions of the will, voluntary and involuntary action in terms of his account of power. The will is 'a *Power* to begin or forbear, continue or end several actions of our minds, and motions of our Bodies, barely by a thought or pre-ference of the mind ordering, or as it were commanding the doing or not doing of such a particular action' (II. XXI. 5. 7–11.: 236). Locke next defines 'voluntary' and 'involuntary'. 'Voluntary' is the actual exercise of the will 'by directing any particular action or its forbearance'. The involuntary is the performing of such acts with-out such a thought or command from the mind.

Locke notes that the powers of perceiving and willing are often called by another name: faculties. He thinks this is unproblematic as long as one is careful about the use of words. There is, however, a problematic use of the term 'faculty'. Locke thinks this arises when we talk about the will as being able to command (see II. XXI. 6. 10–15.: 237). The problematic use is to take the faculties as agents, or we might say as homunculi, that is little people, operating inside us.

Questions

30. What is Locke's distinction between active and passive powers?
31. What is wrong with taking faculties as agents?
32. What are Locke's definitions of voluntary and involuntary action?

Locke thinks that we derive the notions of liberty and necessity from a consideration of the extent of our power over our own actions. In section 8 Locke defines free and not free (see II. XXI. 8. 21–28.: 237).

Locke next goes through a series of cases to show that '*Liberty* cannot be, where there is no Thought, no Volition, no Will; but there may be Will, there may be Volition, where there is no *Liberty*' (II. XXI. 8. 2–4.: 238). His first case is a tennis ball whose motion or rest are both necessary as the tennis ball does not think and so has no volition. In the next case, a man falling from a bridge into water has volition, but is not a free agent because while he wills not to fall, it is not in his power to prevent it. So in this case there is not the right causal connection between the volition not to fall and the motion of his body to make him a free agent. Similarly, a man who strikes himself or his friend by a compulsive motion of his arm that is not in his power to stop and which his thought or volition cannot prevent is not a free agent.

The next case is at II. XXI. 10. 22–32.: 238. Liberty comes from the power either to carry out a volition or not to do so. Locke, though not saying so explicitly, is attacking the doctrine of freedom of the will where the paramount question is about the freedom of volition. Locke thinks that this emphasis on volition is a mistake, for simply having volition is a necessary but not a sufficient condition of liberty. Having the volition and having the power to carry it out (or not) are jointly sufficient for liberty. For a more detailed and precise account of these conditions see Yaffe: 14–15.

The analysis of free will

Locke now turns to the doctrine of the freedom of the will. He rejects freedom of the will. Locke believes that freedom of action is not sufficient to explain free agency. Some additional element is needed (see Yaffe: 19–21: 27). The doctrine of freedom of the will represents one possible account of what the additional element might be. But Locke rejects two different interpretations of freedom of the will in favour of a quite different kind of account.

Locke thinks that clarifying the meaning of the terms and considering the relations between them will avoid much confusion. Locke thinks that clarifying the meaning of the terms will avoid much confusion. He claims that it is incoherent to ask whether the will is free. This is where his previous objection to treating the will as a real being, or a homunculus, has its force. He amplifies this point in sections 18–20. The problem with homunculi, or faculties understood as real beings, is that offering them as explanations turns out to explain nothing.

The will is a faculty and that means simply a power. Freedom is also a power. So in attributing freedom to the will one is attributing a power to a power. But this is as incoherent as to ask if virtue is square. It is a kind of error that Gilbert Ryle in *The Concept of Mind* called a category mistake (Ryle: 16–17). Only agents, substances, can have powers attributed to them. So there can be free agents but not freedom of the will.

What happens, however, in particular cases? Locke replies at II. XXI. 29. 3–16.: 249. This passage, together with what came before, suggests that Locke is a determinist with respect to what he calls volitions, because volitions are caused, and that he is a compatibilist rather than a hard determinist because he believes in free action. Free action means that one can do what one wants without there being any physical constraints preventing one from doing it.

Libertarians claim that the crucial element in free will is being able to do otherwise – to be able to take any of the alternatives that are presented to one. They claim that determinism implies that one could not do otherwise. Compatibilists sometimes offer an account of being able to do otherwise. Locke seems to have such an account although he does not label it in this way. The first stage of his account is to say that we are free insofar as it is in our power to perform any of the actions the will is considering at any particular time.

Locke goes on to claim that the crux of the issue about freedom of the will is the question of whether the will itself is determined or not. His answer comes in several stages. First, he claims: 'That *Willing* or *Volition* being an Action, and Freedom consisting in a power of acting or not acting, *a Man in respect of willing, or the Act of Volition, when any Action in his power is once proposed to his Thoughts, as presently to be done, cannot be free*' (II. XXI. 23. 8–11.: 245). His point is that once the action has been proposed, a man must choose either to perform the action or its negation. He has no choice about having to will something; and having no choice means he is not free.

The next question is: '*Whether a Man be at liberty which of the two he pleases, Motion or Rest*' (II. XXI. 25. 3–4.: 247). Locke claims that the question is absurd and gives his reasons at II. XXI. 25. 4–12.: 247. The point here seems to be that volitions are 'action starters' so if you ask if there is an action starter for the action starter, you involve yourself in an infinite regress. It turns out that in Locke's mature theory volitions are caused not by other volitions but by desires or the uneasiness associated with desire (II. XXI. 29. 3–16.: 249). Volitions thus have both active and passive powers. That something can have both active and passive powers is crucial to Locke's account of free agency and also something he does not explicitly acknowledge. (see Yaffe: 84–5). So, Locke is a determinist and a compatibilist. A compatibilist believes that actions are free when there are no physical constraints such as bars, chains or policemen who prevent one from doing what one desires to do. But, as we have noted above, Locke does not believe that this account of free action is entirely satisfactory. There needs to be an additional element, and that element is not free will on any plausible interpretation. So what, then, is it?

Moral determinism

Locke now takes up a series of questions that are related to moral determinism. One way of characterizing moral determinism is that if one knows that one of the actions one might take will tend towards a greater good, one will always choose that action. Plato was an advocate of moral determinism, arguing in the dialogue *Meno* that everyone seeks the good, and so seeking the good cannot be what distinguishes the virtuous from those who lack virtue. This Platonic view is purely cognitive in the sense that the problem of being virtuous or attaining excellence becomes a problem of knowledge. One may fail in one's efforts to attain the good by mistaking it for what appears to be good, but is in fact not good.

Locke himself had accepted this kind of moral determinism in the first edition of the *Essay* (Yaffe: 32–39). In the second edition, however, he modifies it significantly so as to include a conative or emotional element along with a cognitive one. The emotional element is represented by satisfaction and uneasiness. Of these two, uneasiness tends to be more important. Uneasiness motivates because we always desire to remove pains. The cognitive element is the determination that such an action is either good or evil.

These two elements can conflict, and where they do the emotional or motivational element takes precedence in Locke's modified theory. This takes care of typical counter examples involving weakness of the will or akrasia. These are cases where one does something even though one apparently knows better. Locke claims that a drunkard can know that in the long run drink will ruin his health and quality of life but be driven to drink again by the uneasiness caused by his habits and the desires they engender. Similarly, he thinks that if the greatest good in the long run were really to determine our actions, the desire for salvation would be universally effective, but it is not. It is principally because the modified theory can explain these kinds of cases while the original theory cannot that Locke thinks the modified theory is superior. Let us consider how the emotional and cognitive elements in the theory relate to one another.

Locke talks about the relative motivating power of uneasiness versus some remote and absent good at II. XXI. 45. 27–5.: 261–2. This passage might leave the impression that there is little place for important but remote and absent goods. This is certainly not the case. What role does the contemplation or determination of good and evil play in motivating action? There seems to be a three-step process relating uneasiness, desire and good. We can understand that something is good without desiring it. And if we don't desire it, there will be no uneasiness to motivate us. But when we are contemplating present goods and evils, these pieces go together. We see the good, we feel a desire for it, and that causes a motivating uneasiness from the lack of it. These three elements tend to separate and so cease to motivate us as we begin to deal with more remote and absent goods (see II. XXI. 45. 5–21.: 262).

What ultimately determines us to action is the search for happiness and the avoidance of misery. We are mainly determined by our natural and adopted desires, but contemplation and examination can cause us to seek remoter goods by stimulating in us the desire for them and hence the uneasiness that accompanies desire. Locke thinks that this kind of examination is eminently worth doing. In fact, the process of engaging in this kind of examination makes us free. Locke holds that we have a power to suspend action so that we can contemplate the various types of action we might take and determine which one of them is the most conducive to our happiness. And he thinks it is here that we have what most constitutes freedom – the ability to try to determine by careful examination and inquiry which of our possible actions are most conducive to our happiness and the avoidance of misery (see II. XXI. 47. 12–4.: 263–4).

One might argue that if one is determined by one's vision of what is good then one is not free. Locke disagrees. He remarks that this kind of fair examination 'is so far from being a restraint or diminution of *Freedom*, that it is the very improvement and benefit of it: 'tis not an Abridgment, 'tis the end and use of our *Liberty*, and the farther we are removed from such a determination, the nearer we are to Misery and Slavery' (II. XXI. 48. 5–9.: 264). In fact, it would be an imperfection not to be determined in this way. If we consider 'those Superior beings above us, who enjoy perfect Happiness, we shall have reason to judge that they are *more steadily determined in their choice of Good* than we, and yet we have no reason to think that they are less happy, or less free, than we are'. And Locke thinks that God must also be determined by what is good, but His freedom is not thereby diminished. God presumably has no difficulties in determining what is genuinely good. For us on the other hand rational examination, freedom and the pursuit of happiness go together. Compatibilist free action thus represents one perfection; what completes Locke's account of free agency is the second perfection of being determined by the good. (See the first edition variant of II. XXI. 30 bottom of pp. 251–54). The kind of inquiry exemplified by the *Essay* itself is the key to the discovery of what is for the best and thus human freedom and happiness.

The question then arises as to whether we are free or not to use our power to suspend action. There is very little reason to think that Locke would not hold that this action like all others will be

he same way. What is important is that through
habit we can inculcate in ourselves the practice of
such situations, thus improving our chances of
y happy.

Questions

33. What are Locke's objections to the doctrine of free will?
34. Why is it crucial to Locke's position that volitions have both active and passive powers?
35. What is moral determinism and how does Locke defend it against counter-examples based on the weakness of the will?
36. Given that Locke is a determinist what is his account of freedom and how does it fit with his determinism?

Personal identity and moral relations

Locke's account of identity and personal identity in the chapter 'Of Identity and Diversity' is revolutionary, famous and influential. Locke sets forth a general theory of identity and individuation and then uses this theory to explain his view of personal identity. The discussion of the distinction between the identity of masses of matter and living things provides an analogy for the distinctions that Locke wants to draw between man and person, and person and the soul, or in Locke's clunky phrase, the substance that thinks in us.

Individuation and identity

In sections 1–3 Locke explains the principle of individuation: that two things of the same kind cannot be in the same place at the same time. From this Locke thinks it follows that 'one thing cannot have two beginnings of existence, nor two things one beginning'. He tells us that we have an idea of only three sorts of substances: 1. God, 2. Finite Intelligences and 3. Bodies.

In section 3 he applies this principle to atoms and masses of atoms and then makes a distinction between masses of matter and living things. Masses of atoms or bodies as he also calls them are the same as long as they are composed of the same atoms 'and whilst they exist united together, the Mass consisting of the same Atoms, must be the same Mass, or the same Body, let the parts be never so differently jumbled: But if one of these Atoms be taken away, or one new one added, it is no longer the same Mass, or the same Body' (II. XXVII. 3. 16–20.: 330). He immediately draws the contrast between masses of matter and living things.

> In the state of living Creatures, their identity depends not on a Mass of the same Particles; but on something else. For in them the variation of great parcels of Matter alters not the Identity: An Oak growing from a Plant to a great Tree, and then lopp'd is still the same Oak: And a Colt grows up to a Horse, sometimes fat, sometimes lean, is all the while the same Horse: though in both these Cases, there may be a manifest change of the parts: So that truly they are not either of them the same Mass of Matter, though they be truly one of them the same Oak and the other the same Horse. The reason thereof is, that in these two cases of a Mass of Matter, and a living Body, *Identity* is not applied to the same thing. (II. XXVII. 3. 20–31.: 330)

This sensible distinction that Locke makes between the identity of a mass of matter and that of a living thing causes immediate and severe problems for his theory of identity and individuation. If an atom is a body, and a mass of atoms is also a body, then they clearly belong to Locke's third category of substances, bodies. But if an oak or horse is distinct from the mass that composes it at a certain time, to what category should we assign it? If we say that the horse is a body, but is distinct from the mass that composes it, then we have two things of the same kind in the same place at the same time. Thus we get an immediate violation of Locke's just announced principle of individuation. We might, I suppose, say that they are bodies of different kinds. But while Locke does tell us that in addition to his three kinds of substances there are simple and compounded substances, he does not explicitly say that there are any other kinds of bodies that have characteristics that would allow us to resolve the contradiction. If on the other hand, we say that oaks and horses are not bodies, then what are they? Surely they are not God! This leaves only the category of finite intelligences. One might have thought that finite intelligences were souls. But if that is correct, then this is not a likely category for oak trees or horses. If one then concludes that oaks and horses must not be substances at all, the only alternatives available in Locke's ontology are modes and relations. But, if oaks and horses are supposed to be mixed modes, one is faced with the fact that Locke regularly treats plants and animals as substances in other parts of the *Essay*.

So, while this solution may get us out of the problem in this chapter, it would make Locke's usage inconsistent between II. XXVII and the rest of the *Essay*. There are still other strategies one might try. One might take the distinction that Locke makes between simple and compounded substances and claim that masses of matter are simple substances, while oaks and horses are compounded ones. But this seems counter-intuitive. Surely an atom is a simple substance and a mass of atoms is a compounded one. What is simple about a collection of particles? So this strategy also has its problems. Or one might decide not to take seriously the claim that there are only three categories of substances. But then Locke has not given us a clear account of what it means to be of the same kind and shows no awareness of this problem. Here is a puzzle well worthy of contemplation (see Uzgalis, 1990).

In section 4 Locke makes it clear that living things are individuated by their functional organization and that the purpose of this organization is to preserve the same life through changes in the matter that composes it at any given time. In section 5 he gives essentially the same analysis of the individuation and identity of animals across time. In section 6 he applies this analysis to the definition of man. He writes: '*Man*, consists; *viz* in nothing but the participation of the same continued Life, by constantly fleeting Particles of Matter, in succession vitally united to the same organized Body' (II. XXVII. 6. 35–2.: 331–2). Locke proceeds to argue for this account of the identity of man by noting deficiencies in various competing accounts.

In the following passage, Locke is arguing for his particular account of what a man is, against a competing account.

8. An Animal is a living organized Body; and consequently, the same Animal, as we have observed, is the same continued Life communicated to different Particles of Matter, as they happen, successively to be united to that organiz'd living Body. And whatever is talked of other definitions, ingenious observation puts it past doubt, that the Idea in our minds, of which the Sound *Man* in our mouths is a Sign, is of nothing else but of an Animal of such a certain Form: Since I think I may be confident, that whoever should see a Creature of his own shape, though it

had no more reason all its Life, than a *Cat* or a *Parrot*, would call him still a *Man*; or whoever should hear a *Cat* or a *Parrot* discourse, reason and philosophize, would call or think it nothing but a *Cat* or a *Parrot*; and say the one was a dull, irrational *Man*, and the other a very intelligent, rational *Parrot* (II. XXVII. 8. 35–12.: 332–3).

Locke uses the thought experiment of encountering a rational, talking parrot or cat to make us see that if a creature of another species had this characteristic, we would not call it a 'man'. Thus, the definition of 'man' that Locke is here arguing against is that man is a rational animal. This becomes quite explicit towards the end of section 8.

Man and person
In section 9 Locke offers a definition of person. He defines a person as 'a thinking intelligent Being, that has reason and reflection, and can consider it self as it self, the same thinking thing in different times and places; which it does only by that consciousness, which is inseparable from thinking, and as it seems to me essential to it: It being impossible for any one to perceive, without perceiving that he does perceive' (II. XXVII. 9. 10–16.: 335). Note that reason, which was excluded from the definition of 'man', now finds its proper place here in the definition of person. It looks as if Locke's rational talking cat or parrot might well be a person, although not a man. This suggests that Locke may have been willing to entertain a trans-species conception of person. Locke is clearly drawing a distinction between man and person. 'Man', for instance, is species-specific whereas 'person' is not. It turns out that reflection is just as important as reason in connecting Locke's account of free agency with his account of personal identity, because it ties the volitions that cause the actions for which we are responsible to the self. They are things we are conscious of just as we are conscious of the memories of actions done.

Locke is making the distinction between man and person due to anxieties about the resurrection of the dead on judgement day. He writes:

15. And thus we may without any difficulty to conceive, the same Person at the Resurrection, though in a Body not exactly in

make or parts the same which he had here, the same Consciousness going along with the Soul that inhabits it. But yet the Soul alone in the change of Bodies, would scarce to any one, but to him that makes the Soul the *Man*, be enough to make the same *Man*. For should the Soul of a Prince, carrying with it the consciousness of the Prince's past Life, enter and inform the Body of a Cobler, as soon as deserted by his own Soul, every one sees, he would be the same Person with the Prince, accountable only for the Prince's Actions: but who would say it was the same Man? The Body too goes to the making the Man, and would I guess, to every Body determine the Man in this case, where in the Soul with all its Princely thoughts about it, would not make another Man: But he would be the same Cobler to everyone besides himself (II. XXVII. 15. 4–18.: 340).

The case of the prince and the cobbler is often presented as the first great puzzle case in the literature on personal identity. Should we take memory as the criterion of personal identity or sameness of body? If they are competing with one another as they are in this case, which should we choose? There is the puzzle. But Locke clearly did not intend it as a puzzle case at all. On the contrary, it represented the resolution of an earlier puzzle about the resurrection of the dead at the last judgement. The puzzle has to do with what body a person would have if they had to have the same body at the resurrection as they had in this life. The problems in figuring this out are daunting. From what time period in the person's life should the particles be collected? Should the particles simply come from the body at the moment of death? Or should they come from the period during which the person was sinning? There are other possibilities. Locke goes through all of them with great care in his discussion of this issue with Bishop Stillingfleet (Locke, Vol. IV. 1823: 304–330). But there are telling objections to all of these proposals. Suppose that some of the particles that belonged to one human body also belonged to another, as might well be the case if one of the persons were a cannibal and the other his victim. Who should get the particles that belonged to both of them? By arguing that person and man are different kinds of things, Locke is suggesting that as long as the consciousness is preserved of what acts were done, it does not matter much if one has exactly the same body or not. Thus he resolves this puzzle about the resurrection of the dead. This brings us to yet another distinction that Locke wants to make.

Questions

37. What is Locke's principle of individuation?
38. What is the distinction between the way in which masses of bodies and living things are individuated?
39. What is Locke's definition of 'man' and how does it relate to his definition of 'animal'?
40. What is Locke's definition of 'person' and how does he draw the distinction between man and person?
41. How does the example of the prince and the cobbler illustrate the man/person distinction and what does it explain?

Consciousness and substance

Another important aspect of Locke's definition of 'person' is that it is by consciousness that one knows oneself to be the same thinking thing in different times and places. Ralph Cudworth had only recently given an extensive philosophical treatment of the English word 'consciousness' in his book *The True Intellectual System of the Universe* published in 1678. There are several notable features of Locke's account of consciousness. The most remarkable of these is that consciousness is replacing the soul as the bearer of personal identity.

Locke's contemporary critics, Lee, Sergeant, Clarke, Leibniz and later Berkeley, Butler and Reid, all rejected Locke's substitution of consciousness for substance as the bearer of personal identity. Locke was, it seems clear, keenly aware that what he was proposing was highly controversial. There is an extended discussion in II. XXVII devoted to making the point that it is consciousness and not substance that is the bearer of personal identity. It starts in section 10 and continues through section 14. Locke continues to assert that it is consciousness and not substance that determines personal identity in sections 16, 17, 18 and 19. Section 23 argues that substance cannot unite remote existences into one person while consciousness can. Section 24 argues that without consciousness substance is no part of the self. Thus, most of the chapter after section 10 is concerned with this point. We should begin by wondering what caused Locke to make this highly controversial distinction. The answer I shall give is that Locke's concerns were epistemological. What feature is most likely to secure to us our knowledge of our personal identity? Locke quite simply holds that there is less doubt in regard to consciousness than substance.

Having finished giving his definition of personal identity in terms of consciousness in section 9, Locke opens section 10 with the question of whether it will not only be the same person because consciousness makes it so but also because it is the same substance (see II. XXVII. 10. 29–10.: 335–6). Locke's answer is that it will not necessarily be the same substance. There seem to be some clear attacks on Descartes and the Cartesians here, picking up the argument from II. I. 9–20. Locke goes on to claim that if consciousness were not interrupted – by the ordinary operation of memory and thought, by failure of memory, sleep and so forth – then we might have 'the whole train of our past Actions before our Eyes in one view' and if we had such a view there would be no doubt that we were the same thinking substance (II. XXVII. 10. 34–10.: 335–36). But, apparently, these interruptions of consciousness suggest the possibility that while my consciousness is interrupted, that one substance might be replaced by another.

It is likely that these suspicions about the replacement of one substance by another are reinforced by the analogy between living things and persons. In his analysis of living things, Locke clearly holds that transference of life from one substance to another is not only possible but occurs routinely. He gives the analogy between animal and human identity in section 10 (see II. XXVII. 10. 11–18.: 336). This clearly confirms that masses of matter are both substances and bodies, and that this is what Locke means by saying that the identity of plants and animals does not depend on the unity of substance. It also makes explicit the analogy between life and consciousness, cabbages and kings. The human body is, of course, a living thing. And this is a living thing that is connected with the self in important ways. In section 11, Locke uses this connection to make an explicit argument about the self remaining the same through changes in substance (see II. XXVII. II. 33–5.: 336–7).

We may suppose that this argument is merely the prologue for the questions posed in sections 12 and 13 and thus it seems unlikely that Locke believes that this argument resolves the issue of whether consciousness can be transferred from one thinking substance to another. However, given the difficulties of section 13 in particular, we might want to take a hard look at what Locke has achieved so far. He has provided models and analogies for understanding how an entity can persist and retain its identity through changes of substance. This is in fact the case with a substance which is contingently part of the self: the body itself, both in part and in whole. It remains to be seen whether the relation between persons and the substances that think in us are really like the models of living things, or the man-person relation.

Locke's analogy between the identity of oaks and horses on the one hand and persons on the other suggests that persons can persist through changes in the substances that comprise them at a given time just as oaks and horses do. At the beginning of section 12 of II. XXVII, Locke writes: 'But the Question is: whether if the same Substance, which thinks, be changed, it can be the same Person, or remaining the same, it can be different Persons' (II. XXVII. 12. 10–12.: 337). His answer to both questions is affirmative. This drastically reduces the importance of substance or the soul to personal identity. In effect, Locke attempts to disconnect consciousness from substance by arguing that it is at least possible that one can have the same person even though one does not have the same substance, and also that one can have two or more persons connected with the same substance. The first case suggests that substance is not a necessary condition for personal identity, the second that it is not a sufficient condition. The first case is more controversial since it involves the transference of consciousness or memory from one substance to another. A number of Locke's contemporaries simply denied that this was possible. Samuel Clarke is particularly forceful on this point in his correspondence with Anthony Collins. Joseph Butler and Thomas Reid echoed Clarke in this regard.

On the other hand, Locke treats the presence or absence of consciousness as a necessary and sufficient condition for being the same person. If you are conscious of something someone did a thousand years ago then you are the same as that person. If you really cannot remember some act that was done yesterday, then you are not the person who did that act.

'Person' as a forensic term

Locke's distinction between 'consciousness' and 'substance' is a radical one. I have suggested that Locke's motivation for making this distinction was epistemological. Still, this does not tell us why he is so concerned about knowledge of personal identity. What is the issue? What is at stake? Let us go back to Locke's account of what a person is. Locke says that a person is an intelligent thinking thing that can consider itself the same thinking thing in different times and places. But what is so important about being able to consider oneself the same thinking thing in different times and places? (see II. XXVII. 26. 24–28: 346). One reason why it is important that the self can consider itself the same thinking thing at different times and places is that the nature of the law is to relate rewards or punishments for actions done either in accord with or contrary to the law; and without an intelligent agent being able to grasp that it is the same person who will be punished or rewarded as the agent who is doing the action now, this concept becomes meaningless. To have followed the law and be rewarded for it is to receive pleasure and therefore happiness; to break the law and be punished will result in pain and misery. Thus persons are creatures that can guide themselves towards happiness by calculating that if they obey the law they will be rewarded, causing them to be happy; and that if they fail to obey the law they will be punished, causing them misery. On the other hand, should they make the calculation and deliberately choose to disobey the law, they can later calculate upon their punishment that they are themselves responsible for their own misery. This concept of person as a forensic term might relate to human laws, and Locke very likely has this in mind, but the primary sense is very likely divine law. This interpretation of why being able to know oneself as the same thinking thing in different times and places nicely connects Locke's account of personal identity with his account of volitions and free action in Book II chapter XXI and with his account of morality in Book II chapter XXVIII. One perceptive connection is provided by Locke's remark that a concern for happiness is the unavoidable concomitant of consciousness (see II. XXVII. 26. 35–5.: 346–7), while his theory of volition explains how we are to achieve this, and the portion of his account dealing with morality in terms of divine law along with its punishments and rewards accords with both (Yaffe: 119–39).

In the discussion of the prince and the cobbler example in section 2, we saw that one of the motivations for Locke's distinction between man and person was that he could resolve puzzles about what happens at the resurrection of the dead on judgement day. Locke's account of personal identity in terms of consciousness rather than the soul is clearly related to another aspect of judgement day – that of punishment being meted out for sins committed and rewards being given for good deeds. Put simply, Locke's doctrine is that you cannot be justly punished or rewarded for actions which you cannot remember doing. There is an essential connection between knowing that you did the action and the pleasure or pain received for performing that action. If this essential connection is severed, Locke holds that justice fails. This largely explains Locke's narrow focus on consciousness as a device for action appropriation. There are interesting analogies here between the term *conscience* and *consciousness*. They both have the same etymology: '*con*', together, and '*scire*', to know. This suggests that we have two persons knowing the same thing: an actor who performs the action and a witness who sees the action performed and who remembers and judges. Combine these two roles in the same person and you get consciousness and conscience.

There is definitely something in this. Surely we ordinarily expect that when someone is rewarded or punished, they will know that they did the action for which they are being rewarded or punished, and know it, as it were, from the inside, not by being told or supplied with the evidence that shows that they did it. Dog trainers insist that it is pointless to punish a dog whom you discover has eaten holes in your beautiful new couch sometime earlier in the day, precisely because the dog will not put together the knowledge that it did the 'crime' with the knowledge that it is being punished now for committing it. It does not know itself after the event as the same chewing thing that happily defaced your sofa. It thus serves no good purpose to punish the animal, precisely because it cannot operate the machinery of the law and so will neither be deterred from similar actions in the future nor improved in other ways. It must be steered towards happiness and away from misery in some other way. The ideal situation for stopping such behaviour in dogs is to punish them while they are committing the offending act. This shows the importance not just of consciousness but also of memory of a particular kind.

Clearly, however, whatever its merits, there are difficulties with Locke's doctrine. Both Molyneaux and Leibniz (when he came to write the *New Essays*) point out serious difficulties. It seems perfectly possible that while I don't remember some stretch of my life someone else might have compelling evidence that it was I who performed some action or other. This may be a borderline case in terms of Locke's central intuition about justice and consciousness but it seems perfectly possible. It also seems that Locke's account of justice requires perfect recall of all actions that are subject to punishment or reward. This seems like a distinctly non-naturalistic account of memory.

In section 20 Locke takes up a supposition and an objection based on this supposition that shows us that he is aware of some of the obvious difficulties with his position, and tells us his answer, 'suppose, I wholly lose the memory of some parts of my Life, beyond a possibility of retrieving them, so that perhaps I shall never be conscious of them again; yet am I not the same Person, that did those Actions, had those Thoughts, that I was once conscious of, though I have now forgot them?' (II. XXVII. 20. 23–28.: 342). Locke's response to this objection is that we must carefully consider what 'I' stands for, and that while 'I' usually stands both for the same man and the same person, in this case what we will have is the same man but not the same person. He continues:

But if it be possible for the same man to have distinct incommunicable consciousness at different times, it is past doubt the same Man would at different times make different Persons; which, we see, is the sense of Mankind in the solemnest Declaration of their Opinions, Humane laws not punishing the *Mad man* for the *Sober man's* Actions, nor the *Sober man* for what the *Mad man* did, thereby making them two Persons; which is somewhat explained by our way of speaking in *English*, when we say such an one *is not himself*, or is *besides himself*; in which Phrases it is insinuated, as if those who now, or, at least, first used them, thought, that *self* was changed, the *self* same Person was not in the Man. (II. XXVII. 20. 31–4: 342–3.)

So Locke holds that if I cannot remember, beyond the possibility of recall, something which 'I' did, then it was done by a different person, even if that person happened to be operating in the same living human body in which I presently operate. He also thinks that this distinction between man and person and the associated claims about consciousness and memory are represented both in ordinary language and the practice of law.

Questions

42. What reasons does Locke give for replacing substance with consciousness as the bearer of personal identity?
43. How does the identity of plants and animals provide an analogy for important features of the identity of persons?
44. What does Locke mean in saying that 'person' is a forensic term?
45. Do you think that Locke's claim that we must remember what we did in order to be justly punished for it is plausible?

Relations and moral relations

Having established the forensic character of personal identity, Locke proceeds in the next chapter to discuss relations and in particular moral relations. Locke remarks that having compared things in terms of time, place and causality, there are an infinity of other such comparisons possible of which he proposes to mention a few. He begins with two things that are compared in respect of the same simple idea, one being whiter or larger or sweeter than another. A second relation is that of considering the origin or beginning of some thing, and because such origins cannot later be altered 'make the Relations, depending thereon, as lasting as the Subjects to which they belong; v.g. *Father* and *Son*, *Brothers*, *Cousin-Germans*, etc' (II. XXVIII. 2. 13–15.: 349). These relations are in a certain sense arbitrary because we pick them out and name them in cases that are important to us but not in cases that are not. We are concerned with human relations, but not so much with the corresponding ones in other animals. This leads Locke to remark that this phenomenon may 'give us some light into the different state and growth of Languages, which being suited only to the Convenience of Communication, are proportioned to the Notions Men have, and the commerce of Thoughts familiar amongst them; and not to the Reality or Extent of Things, nor to the various Respects might be found among them . . .' (II. XXVIII. 2. 32–37.: 349). Here we get a clear foretaste of the position that Locke is going to take about the human origins of language in Book III of the *Essay*.

The third class of relations that Locke considers are moral relations. If being a person implies having the powers and capacities to operate the laws, and the laws connect reward and punishment to the deeds done at a particular time and place and make such rewards and punishments just, the most important part of Locke's account of morality is primarily in terms of law. Thus, in section 5 of II. XXVIII he writes:

> Good and Evil ... are nothing but Pleasure and Pain, or that which occasions or procures Pleasure or Pain to us. *Morally Good or Evil* then, is only the Conformity or Disagreement of our Voluntary actions to some Law, whereby Good or Evil is drawn on us, by the Will and Power of the Law-maker; which Good and Evil, Pleasure or Pain, attending our Observance or Breach of the Law, by the decree of the Law-maker, is that what we call *Reward* and *Punishment*. (II. XXVIII. 5. 17–24.: 351).

He then goes on to distinguish three kinds of rules with different kinds of punishments and rewards. He argues that rules or laws without rewards and punishments to enforce them make no sense. The three sorts of rules are divine law, civil law and the law of opinion or reputation. Divine law comes either 'by the light of Nature, or the voice of Revelation' (II. XXVIII. 8. 15–16.: 352). Understanding this law is important not simply because the law-maker has the power to enforce such law with rewards and punishments of infinite weight, but because 'He has the Wisdom and Goodness to direct our actions to what is best ...' (II. XXVIII. 8. 19–20.: 352). Thus, the proper use of reason to discover the natural law fits together nicely with our morally determined nature and the nature of consciousness itself with its concomitant desires to pursue pleasure and avoid pain in order to achieve happiness.

In the section on civil law we can see a connection with Locke's *Second Treatise of Government* (Locke, 1980). In this section, Locke claims that the civil law is made by the Commonwealth for the purpose of protecting the lives, liberties and possessions of those who live in it, and the penalty for disobeying the law is to take away the life, liberty or goods from him who disobeys. In the *Second Treatise* it is plain that the powers of a legitimate Commonwealth are derived from the natural law and so the second kind of moral rules echo the first.

The third kind of rule, that of approbation of virtue and disapprobation of vice, are pretended to stand for actions that are 'in their own nature right and wrong: And so far as they really are so applied, they are so far coincident with the *divine Law* above mentioned' (II. XXVIII. 10. 5–8.: 353). Locke says that such actions are supposed or pretended to be in their own nature right and wrong because, in fact, these are actions whose rightness and wrongness is determined differently in different countries and societies. This rule of reputation and opinion is enforced by the praise or blame distributed by people in these different countries or societies.

Judgements about ideas and the Association of ideas

At the end of chapter XXIX Locke notes that he has completed his investigation into the origin of ideas. He has considered the origins of simple and complex ideas and how the complex ones are divided into those of modes, substances and relations. Still, there is more to be said about ideas. Book II of the Essay comes to a close with a series of chapters – XXIX through XXXII – that elucidate various distinctions we make about ideas. Ideas can be clear or obscure, distinct or confused, real or fantastical, adequate or inadequate, or true or false. The terms for these distinctions may well come mostly from Descartes, and even some of the analogies used to explain them, but the distinctions being drawn are not exactly the same. Distinctness in Descartes, for example, has to do with whether all the simple ideas in a complex idea are clear, whereas for Locke it is possible for one simple idea to be clear and distinct. Book II ends with a discussion of the association of ideas.

Locke's account of the association of ideas in the final chapter of Book II of the *Essay* is negative. Hume was later to make a positive account of the association of ideas a central feature of his science of man. Locke's account of the association of ideas treats it as a form of madness that contrasts with the association of ideas produced by reason. He thinks it can be called prejudice and that it is sometimes inculcated by education, but he thinks that this analysis does not go deep enough. Prejudice is expressed in the association of ideas that have no real connection with one another. It is a form of madness to which even good and sober people are susceptible. The association of ideas condemned by Locke involves the accidental rather than the natural correspondence and connection of ideas that reason makes us aware of. Locke claims that 'this wrong Connexion in our Minds of *Ideas* in themselves, loose and independent one of another, has such an influence, and is of so great a force to set us awry in our Actions, as well Moral as Natural, Passions, Reasoning and Notions themselves, that, perhaps there is not any one thing that deserves more to be looked after' (II. XXIX. 9. 27–31.: 397). Locke holds, for example, that the difference between the different schools of philosophers is very likely a result of the association of ideas.

Questions

46. In what ways does Locke's account of moral relations and moral action fit together with his account of volition, moral determinism and personal identity?
47. How plausible do you find Locke's account of the association of ideas as the root of prejudice?

BOOK III OF THE *ESSAY*

The organization of Book III

Book III begins with a discussion of words and language, then progresses to general terms (chapters I–III), the names of simple ideas, and the names of mixed modes and relations (chapters IV and V). After this comes the long chapter on the names of substances (chapter VI) and a very short chapter on particles and then a discussion of abstract and concrete terms (chapter VIII). After this Locke turns to the imperfections and abuses of words (chapters IX and X) and then in chapter XI the remedies for these imperfections and abuses.

Language and knowledge

Locke devotes Book III of *An Essay Concerning Human Understanding* to language. This is a strong indication that Locke thinks issues about language were of considerable importance in attaining knowledge. At the beginning of the Book he notes the importance to knowledge of abstract general ideas. These serve as categories under which we rank the vast multitude of specific cases. Thus, abstract ideas and classification are of central importance in Locke's discussion of language. We may find it a little disappointing that in using his 'plain historical method' Locke does not pay more attention to the profound effects of language acquisition. The acquisition of language is surely a huge progression in the development of children. Locke says very little about it. Given his view that

we are born with the powers to manipulate ideas such as comparison and abstraction, while the content of our ideas comes from
experience, it is possible that Locke might have been willing to
accept a view like that of Noam Chomsky that our capacity for
language acquisition is innate. On Chomsky's view, if syntactic
structures are taken to be innate, and as long as such structures
have no semantic content, they would not violate Locke's claim that
none of the semantic content of our knowledge is innate (Chomsky,
1957).

There is a clear connection between Book II and III in that Locke
claims that words stand for ideas. In his discussion of language,
Locke distinguishes words according to the categories of ideas established in Book II of the *Essay*. So there are ideas of substances,
simple modes, mixed modes, relations and so on. It is in this context
that Locke makes the distinction between real and nominal essences
alluded to above in the discussion of substances. Because of his
focus on the role that terms about kinds of things play in classification, Locke pays vastly more attention to nouns than to verbs. He
also recognizes that not all words relate to ideas; there are the many
particles, words that signify the connexion that the Mind gives to
Ideas, or Propositions, one with another (III. VII. 1.: 471). Still, it is
the relation of nouns and ideas that receives the bulk of Locke's
attention in Book III.

Locke wrote that '*Words, in their primary or immediate Signification, stand for Nothing, but the* Ideas *in the Mind of him that
uses them . . .*' (III. II. 2. 21–22.: 405). Norman Kretzmann calls this
'the least unsatisfactory' of Locke's formulations of his main semantic thesis (Kretzmann: 126). Kretzmann notes that this thesis
has often been criticized as a classic blunder in semantic theory.
Thus Mill, for example, wrote, 'When I say, "the sun is the cause of
the day", I do not mean that my idea of the sun causes or excites in
me the idea of day' (Kretzmann: 125). This criticism of Locke's
account of language parallels the 'veil of perception' critique of his
account of perception and suggests that Locke is not distinguishing
the meaning of a word from its reference. Kretzmann, however,
argues persuasively that Locke distinguishes between meaning and
reference and that ideas provide the meaning but not the reference
of words. Thus, the line of criticism represented by the quotation
from Mill is ill-founded. Still, there are peculiarities about Locke's
views about reference that we must consider in due course.

In addition to the kinds of ideas noted above, there are also particular and abstract ideas. Particular ideas have in them the ideas of particular places and times which limit the application of the idea to a single individual, while abstract general ideas leave out the ideas of particular times and places in order to allow the idea to apply to other similar qualities or things. There has been considerable philosophical and scholarly debate about the nature of the process of abstraction and Locke's account of it. Berkeley argued that the process as Locke conceived it is incoherent. This is in part because Berkeley is an imagist – he believes that all ideas are images. If one is an imagist, it becomes impossible to imagine an abstract idea of a triangle that could include in it, for example, the idea of a right-angled triangle and that of an equilateral triangle which cannot have a right angle in it. What image could combine these two? Michael Ayers argues that Locke too was an imagist (Ayers, 1991: 44–51). This would make Berkeley's criticism of Locke very much to the point. Ayers' claim, however, has been disputed. Locke abetted Berkeley at times by formulating his account of abstraction in a confused way. The process of abstraction is of considerable importance to human knowledge. Locke thinks that most of the words we use are general (III. I. 1.: 409). Clearly, it is only general ideas and words that refer to sorts that can serve in a classificatory scheme.

Questions

1. If all things are particulars, why does Locke think that general words and ideas play such an important part in human knowledge?
2. In what way is Book III clearly connected to Book II?
3. What is Locke's main semantic thesis?
4. In what ways does the kind of criticism offered by Mill of Locke's account of the relation of ideas to words parallel the criticism of Locke's account of the relation of ideas to perception in Book II?

Simple ideas and definitions; modes and relations

In chapter III of Book III, Locke makes the point that as far as he knows no one previously had a good way of distinguishing between words that could be defined and those that could not. He claims that all simple ideas are known ostensively and so are not capable of definition. There are some interesting examples. He argues that the corpuscularians who try to define 'motion' simply substitute a synonym for it when they define motion as 'the passing from one place to another'. All complex ideas, on the other hand, are definable in terms of the simple ideas of which they are composed and can be understood as long as all the simple ideas are within the experience of the person trying to understand. This distinction seems like a nice step in Locke's project of determining what we can know and what we cannot know.

The distinction between modes and substances is surely one of the most important in Locke's philosophy. In contrast with substances, modes are dependent existences – they can be thought of as the ordering of substances. These are technical terms for Locke, so we should see how they are defined. Locke writes: 'First, *Modes* I call such complex *Ideas*, which however compounded, contain not in themselves the supposition of subsisting by themselves; such are the words signified by the Words *Triangle, Gratitude, Murther, etc.*' (II. XII. 4.: 165). Locke goes on to distinguish between simple and mixed modes (see II. XII. 4. 1–6.: 165).

When we make ideas of modes, the mind is again active, but the archetype is in our mind. The question becomes whether things in the world fit our ideas, not whether our ideas correspond to the nature of things in the world. Because this is so, our ideas are adequate. Thus we define 'bachelor' as an unmarried, adult, male human being. If we find that someone does not fit this definition, this does not reflect badly on our definition; it simply means that that individual does not belong to the class of bachelors. Modal ideas seem to have some affinities with Hume's relations among ideas and Kant's category of the *analytic a priori*.

Modes give us the ideas of mathematics, of morality, of religion and politics and indeed of human conventions in general as well as types of states and events, such as gratitude, jealousy, a procession and a murder. Since these modal ideas are not only made by us, but serve as standards that things in the world either fit or do not fit and thus belong or do not belong to, ideas of modes are clear and distinct, adequate and complete. Thus in modes we get the real and nominal essences combined. One can give precise definitions of mathematical terms (that is, give necessary and sufficient conditions) and one can give deductive demonstrations of mathematical truths. In section 16 of Book III, chapter XI, Locke says that morality too is capable of deductive demonstration. Though pressed by his friend William Molyneaux to produce such a demonstrative morality, Locke never did so.

The terms of political discourse contain some similar features. When Locke defines the states of nature, slavery and war in the *Second Treatise of Government*, for example, we are presumably getting precise modal definitions from which one can deduce consequences. It is possible, however, that with politics we are getting a study that requires both experience as well as the deductive modal aspect.

It turns out, however, that when Locke comes to consider the imperfections of words, many of the apparent epistemological superiorities of modes surprisingly turn into problems.

Questions

5.   What is the distinction that Locke draws between words that can be defined and those that cannot?
6.   What is it about modal ideas that make them capable of demonstration?

Names of substances

The discussion of classification begins in earnest with chapter VI, on the theme of the names of substances. Locke begins the chapter by remarking that: '*The common names of Substances*, as well as other general Terms, *stand for Sorts*, which is nothing else but the being made signs of such complex *Ideas*, wherein several particular Substances, do or might agree, by virtue of which, they are capable to be comprehended in one common Conception, and be signified by one Name' (III. VI. 1. 28–3.: 438–9). Locke then proceeds to give an example of the sun, which, if abstracted to include more than a single substance, gives us the sort 'star'. This example embodies one of the main themes of the chapter, that is: 'how much the Sorts, or, if you please, the *Genera* and *Species* of Things (for those Latin terms signify to me no more than the English word Sort) depend on such Collections of Ideas, as Men have made, and not on the real Nature of Things: since 'tis not impossible, but that in Propriety of Speech, that might be a Sun to one, that is a Star to another' (III. VI. 1. 10–15.: 439). Locke is beginning an argument against the

Aristotelians and the scholastics who believed that our classificatory systems do mirror the real divisions of things in nature.

Locke next defines the term 'essence' and distinguishes between what he calls the nominal essence and the real atomic constitution of things. 'The measure and boundary of each Sort, or *Species*, whereby it is constituted that particular Sort, and distinguished from others, is that we call its *Essence*, which is nothing but that *abstract* Idea *to which the Name is annexed*: So that everything contained in that *Idea*, is essential to that Sort' (III. VI. 2. 16–20.: 439). The abstract idea is the collection of simple ideas we have decided are parts of the idea of that sort of thing. These ideas we get from experience. Locke calls such a general idea that picks out a sort, the *nominal essence* of that sort.

Locke tells us that the nominal essences of things depend on the atomic constitution of those things. All the apparent properties of gold that are a part of its nominal essence, such as its colour, fusibility, weight, malleability and so on, depend on the atomic constitution of gold. Since the atomic constitution of things is even more fundamentally important than the nominal essence, one might think that Locke would call this the essence. He is indeed willing to call it the real essence, but he is at pains to argue that the atomic constitutions of things cannot provide the meaning of our general terms.

One strand of the argument is that we simply don't know the real essences of material substances, so they cannot provide the meanings of our general terms. He makes this point in reference to the familiar sort 'man'. He points out that if we take voluntary motion, with sense and reason joined to a body of a certain shape as the nominal essence of man, no one will mistake these for the atomic constitution of man. If we had the knowledge of the real essence of man that God or the angels have we would have a quite different idea from the one that is now contained in our definition (see III. VI. 3. 10–15.: 440).

In this passage Locke is using the great clock at Strasbourg, a mechanical marvel of its time, built between 1570 and 1574, to make clear the vast difference between knowing the real and nominal essences of things. At the ground level of the clock, in the centre, there was a three-foot astronomical globe with a twenty-four hour movement, and behind that a ten-foot rotating calendar and clock recording the years, months, days, nights, equinoxes and festivals. Above this presided the titular deity for the day of the week. Two fixed side panels recorded the eclipses. At the first-floor level the central astrolabe plotted the position of the planets in the zodiac and marked the hours, while the dial at the front of the balustrade showed minutes and quarters. The dial above the astrolabe depicted the current phase of the moon. At the third level, rotating jacks struck the quarter hours and Death the hours. The whole structure was elaborately sculpted and painted with religious, allegorical and secular motifs. There was a second tower that housed the weights and was surmounted by a mechanical cockerel, which sprang into life after each carillon.

A variety of philosophers in the seventeenth and eighteenth centuries used the great clock at Strasbourg as an analogue or model for the universe, which suggested that God was a great clockmaker. So Locke is saying that while we can come and be astonished by the outward appearances of things (as the gazing rustic is by the outward marvels of the clock), we can never get at the inner springs and wheels (the organization of the atomic constitution of material substances), which are known only to the clockmaker (God) and his assistants (the angels). The analogy is also worth noting, because it resonates with Locke's endorsement of natural religion and the teleological argument that we shall come to in the discussion of the abuses of language.

In section 4 Locke argues that individuals viewed without reference to a sort have no properties that are essential to them. Locke regularly takes 'inseparable' as a synonym for 'essential'. Taking himself as an example, he points out that his colour, shape, reason, memory, sense, understanding and life are all properties that can either be radically altered or that he can lose altogether. So, he argues, none of these properties are essential until the mind refers them to some sort. Only when John Locke is considered as a man does losing reason or memory or life mean that he has lost some essential property: he would no longer be counted as belonging to the sort 'man'. So, the only basis for denominating some property as essential is relative to our abstract idea of a sort.

What about real essences then? Apart from their fundamental explanatory character, why should we call the atomic constitution of a material object its real essence since it does not determine our classificatory system? Locke makes a distinction between the real essence as determined by a nominal essence and the atomic constitution of an individual. The properties in the real essence cause the apparent ones we perceive and use for classification. So although we do not experience them directly, they may legitimately be called the real essence.

Questions

7. How does Locke define 'essence', 'nominal essence', and real essence'?
8. What is the point that Locke is making with the analogy between the great clock at Strasbourg and the universe?
9. How do sorts relate to essential properties? What point does Locke make about his own properties to explain this?

Abstraction, classification and anti-essentialism

One of the central issues in Book III has to do with classification. On what basis do we divide things into kinds and organize those kinds into a system of species and genera? In the Aristotelian and scholastic tradition that Locke rejects, necessary properties are those that an individual must have in order to exist and continue to exist. These contrast with accidental properties. Accidental properties are those that an individual can gain and lose and yet continue existing. If a set of necessary properties is shared by a number of individuals, that set of properties constitutes the essence of a natural kind. The aim of Aristotelian science is to discover the essences of natural kinds. Kinds can then be organized hierarchically into a classificatory system of species and genera. This classification of the world by natural kinds will be unique and privileged because it alone corresponds to the structure of the world. This doctrine of essences and kinds is often called Aristotelian essentialism. Locke, as should already be evident, rejects a variety of aspects of this doctrine. He rejects the notion that an individual has an essence apart from being treated as belonging to a kind. He also rejects the claim that there is a single classification of things in nature that the natural philosopher should seek to discover. He holds that there are many possible ways to classify the world, each of which might be particularly useful depending on one's purposes. From section 10 through 24 Locke offers a variety of considerations that argue that there are no clear-cut boundaries to species in nature, including appeals to the venerable doctrine of the Great Chain of Being, accounts of remarkable borderline cases between species and so on.

Question

10. How does the distinction between essential and accidental properties of individuals help elucidate the Aristotelian essentialism that Locke rejects?

Locke's pragmatism

Locke holds that language was made for communication and quick dispatch of affairs. Locke's pragmatic account of language and the distinction between nominal and real essences constitutes an anti-essentialist alternative to Aristotelian essentialism and its correlative account of the classification of natural kinds. He claims that there are no fixed boundaries in nature to be discovered – that there are no clear demarcation points between species; there are always borderline cases.

There is scholarly debate over whether Locke's view is that this lack of fixed boundaries is true on both the level of appearances and nominal essences, and atomic constitutions and real essences, or on the level of nominal essences alone. On the first view, Locke holds that there are no natural kinds on either the level of appearance or atomic reality; while according to the second view, Locke thinks that there are real natural kinds on the atomic level, but that we cannot get at them or know what they are. On either of these interpretations, the real essence cannot provide the meaning of names of substances. In the first case, there is only an epistemological problem that prevents us from discovering the Aristotelian natural kinds in nature. On the second view, there are both epistemological and metaphysical reasons for rejecting the Aristotelian doctrine of natural kinds. (See Uzgalis, 1988).

By contrast, the ideas that we use to make up our nominal essences come to us from experience. Locke claims that the mind is active in making our ideas of sorts and that there are so many properties to choose from that it is possible for different people to make quite different ideas of the essence of a particular substance. This has given some commentators the impression that the making of sorts is utterly arbitrary and conventional for Locke and that there is no basis for criticizing a particular nominal essence.

Sometimes Locke says things that might suggest this (see, for example, III. IX. 12. 22–30.: 482–3). But he also points out that the making of nominal essences is constrained both by usage (where words stand for ideas that are already in use) and by the fact that substance words are supposed to copy the properties of the substances they refer to.

Let us begin with the usage of words. It is important that in a community of language users words with agreed meanings be used. If this condition is met, it facilitates the chief end of language, which is communication. If one fails to use words with the meanings that most people attach to them, one will fail to communicate effectively with others, thus defeating the main purpose of language. It should also be noted that for Locke traditions of usage can be modified. Otherwise we would not be able to improve our knowledge and understanding by getting more clear and determinate ideas.

In the making of the names of substances there is a period of discovery as the abstract general ideas are put together (such as the discovery of violets or gold) and then the naming of those ideas and then their introduction into language. Language itself is viewed as an instrument for carrying on the mainly prosaic activities of everyday life. Ordinary people are the chief makers of language (see III. VI. 25. 29–3.: 452–3). These ordinary people use a few apparent qualities, mainly ideas of secondary qualities, to make ideas and words that will serve their purposes.

Natural philosophers come along later to try to determine if the connections between properties that ordinary folk have put together in a particular idea in fact exist in nature. Natural philosophers are seeking to find the necessary connections between properties in nature. Still even scientists, in Locke's view, are restricted to using observable (and mainly secondary) qualities to categorize things in nature. Sometimes the scientists may find that the ordinary folk have erred, as when they called whales 'fish'. A whale is not a fish, as it turns out, but a mammal. There is a characteristic group of qualities that fish have which whales do not have. There is a characteristic group of qualities that mammals possess in common with whales. To classify a whale as a fish is therefore a mistake. (This is not a Lockean example, but he gives a precisely similar one about whether bats are birds at III. XI. 7. 7–19.: 511). Similarly, we might make an idea of gold that only includes being a soft metal and gold in colour. If so, we would be unable to distinguish between gold and fool's gold. Thus, since it is the mind that makes complex ideas (they are 'the workmanship of the understanding'), one is free to put together any combination of ideas one wishes and call it what one will. But the product of such work is open to criticism, either on the grounds that it does not conform to already current usage, or that it inadequately represents the archetypes that it is supposed to mirror in the world (see II. XXXII. 18. 20–25.: 391). We engage in such criticism in order to improve human understanding of the material world and thus the human condition.

In an interesting essay on Locke's philosophy of language, Paul Guyer argues that Locke's anti-essentialism derives from Locke's account of abstraction alone. Guyer writes: 'Locke's conclusion that species are the workmanship of the understanding is derived solely from the logic of his analysis of the force of general terms, and has nothing to do with substantive claims about the kinds of similarities that actually obtain among individuals in nature or with specific limits in our scientific knowledge of natural objects' (Guyer: 130).

Guyer's point is that on Locke's account of abstraction we are forced to choose among a multitude of possible similarities and differences in making the particular abstract idea that we are making. So, any general idea must be the workmanship of the understanding. Later in the article Guyer writes: 'Locke never denies that there are objective and perfectly well defined similarities and differences among particular objects at any level of description, he merely argues that no such similarities or differences constitute the boundaries of species unless we choose to use them for that purpose' (Guyer: 137). For this reason, Guyer holds that Locke's 'more detailed discussion of the names of substances' has misled his contemporaries and recent commentators. This is because Locke actually does address the similarities and differences between individuals on the macroscopic and microscopic levels, whereas Guyer holds that there is no reason for him to do this. But there is reason to think that Locke may need to do this.

Once one recognizes the point that on Locke's account of abstraction we must choose which similarities and differences to use in the making of the idea of a species, the next question is presumably on what basis are we to make that decision? Perhaps the decision is arbitrary or perhaps it is determined by our various purposes. Or the Aristotelians could argue that we should choose a system of classification that best corresponds to the actual divisions in nature. Guyer's interpretation would make our choices arbitrary. But, there are two points worth making against this view. First, Locke tells us that in creating our ideas of substances we try to make them fit with what is out there. Substances are the archetypes and we try to make our ideas correspond to those archetypes. Thus, even though any person is free to put together whatever simple ideas they please in making their idea of a substance, we will judge the adequacy of such ideas on the basis of how well they correspond to their archetypes. The same sort of remark will then apply to our classification of substances. This being so, if there existed the natural kinds that the Aristotelians imagined and we were able to discover them, we would have good reason to choose to adopt a classificatory system based on these natural kinds rather than some other system. It is for this reason that Locke argues against the Aristotelians. And so all of Locke's talk about the Great Chain of Being and the rest that Guyer takes to be misleading comes back and has a proper place in Locke's argument once again. Locke holds that the Aristotelians and scholastics are wrong when they claim that there is a classificatory scheme that uniquely corresponds to the divisions in nature. Because this is so, we should not look for such a scheme. In fact, this argument continues into Book IV where Locke argues that the Aristotelians cannot effectively deal with borderline cases (IV. IV. 13–18.: 569–73).

Questions

11. Who are the original makers of languages and for what purposes do they make them?
12. What constraints are there on the use of words, especially names of substances?
13. How might Locke's view of abstraction contribute to his anti-essentialism?
14. What arguments does Locke give against the claim that there are clear boundaries between species in nature?

The imperfections and abuses of language

The imperfections of words

We use words and language to recollect our ideas and to talk to ourselves as well as to others. Locke claims that there are two kinds of public discourse. The first he calls civil discourse and the second philosophical discourse. Civil discourse is the language of the ordinary affairs of life and the fact that our words have no settled signification causes us fewer problems here than in philosophical discourse. Philosophical discourse is intended 'to convey the precise Notions of Things, and to express, in general Propositions, certain undoubted truths, which the Mind may rest upon, and be satisfied with, in its search after true Knowledge' (III. IX. 3. 27–30.: 476). It is these philosophical uses against which we measure the perfection or imperfection of words. Since words are sounds arbitrarily assigned to stand for ideas, one sound is just as good as another. So, the problem of the imperfection of words lies mainly with the ideas and not with the sounds. 'The chief End of Language in Communication being to be understood, Words serve not well for that end, neither in civil nor in philosophical Discourse, when any word does not excite in the Hearer, the same *Idea* which it stands for in the Mind of the Speaker (III. IX. 4. 33–1.: 476–7). We often learn words by hearing the sounds and do not enquire what ideas are included in the meaning of the word. We can then come to think we understand when we do not. Similarly, when different people include different ideas in what they mean by a given word, while assuming that everyone means the same thing, communication fails and many disputes arise that appear to be about substantive issues, but are in fact about the meaning of words.

The main imperfection of language that Locke is concerned with is that people use words without being clear about what ideas they stand for (III. IX. 4. 33–8.: 476–7). This problem comes in degrees. We are least likely to make mistakes with simple ideas because a simple idea is easily acquired and retained. Next come simple modes, especially those of figure and number, because we have such clear and distinct ideas that we do not mistake seven for some other number or a triangle for a square. Next we have mixed modes that contain only a few obvious ideas and usually have names whose meaning is reasonably clear. It is when we get to mixed modes with many ideas in them, and finally ideas of substances, that problems with the meanings of words become much more significant.

There are several problems with mixed modes. The first is that such ideas are often very complex. As a result, in making such ideas people often include different ideas. This is, Locke says, particularly true of moral ideas (III. IX. 6. 8–17.: 478). The second is that once they are created, it may well be difficult for others to determine what ideas were originally included in them. This is because there is no standard in nature to which the idea may be referred. This makes determining the meaning of ancient texts such as the Bible difficult (III. IX. 9. 27–38.: 480). Common usage affords some assistance in determining the meaning of mixed modes, but this is largely true of civil discourse and is of little use in philosophical discourse (III. IX. 8. 14–34.: 479). Another problem with mixed modes, and moral terms especially, is that children regularly learn them by hearing the words and are then 'either beholden to the explication of others, or (which happens for the most part) are left to their own observation or industry ...' (III. IX. 10. 7–9.: 480). So moral words in particular tend in the mouths of most people to be bare sounds, or loose and undetermined, and so their meaning is obscure and confused. Others who give more attention to such terms may well find that the meanings they assign to them are different from those assigned by other people. And thus one can easily see in debates about such terms as honour, faith, grace, religion, church that people simply do not mean the same things by the terms they are debating, and so the debate is largely useless (III. IX. 10. 17–24.: 480).

Locke tells us that if the names of mixed modes are doubtful because there is no fixed pattern for them in nature, the names of substances are doubtful for a contrary reason (III. IX. 11. 20–24.: 481). There are two problems with the names of substances. The first is that the meaning of the word has reference to a standard – an external archetype in the case of material substances – that is not easily known. If the standard is supposed to be the real essence, then it is likely not to be known at all. The second problem is that if we take the simple ideas that co-exist in a substance as the standard, this may well still give us various and uncertain ideas and names of substances. This is because there are so many ideas that can be included in the meaning of an idea of substance, that depending on differing amounts of care, industry and observation, people are quite likely to produce different ideas, all of which have just as much right as the others to be regarded as the meaning of 'gold' or 'antimony'.

At the end of the chapter on the 'Imperfections of Words', Locke returns to the Bible and argues that the amount of commentary on the Old and New Testaments proves the difficulties involved in determining the meaning of words. He contrasts the difficulties of interpreting the Bible with the plainness of the proofs of God's existence and the obedience due him that come from natural religion, that is the study of nature (see III. IX. 23. 12–19.: 490).

Abuses of words

The abuses of language are the 'willful Faults and Neglects, which men are Guilty of, in this way of Communication, whereby they render these signs less clear and distinct in their signification, than naturally they need to be' (III. X. 1. 22–25.: 490). The first of these abuses is to use words with no clear and distinct ideas attached to them. He calls these 'insignificant terms'. Locke has in mind here the jargon of the schools. These are coined 'either affecting something singular, and out of the way of common apprehensions, or to support some strange Opinions, or to cover some Weakness of their Hypothesis' (III. X. 2. 2–5.: 491). The next abuse is to take important words that have a common usage and use them without any distinct meaning at all. In civil discourse this results in an advantage for those who abuse words in this way: 'That as in such Discourse, they are seldom in the right, so they are seldom to be convinced, that they are in the wrong; it being all one to go about to draw those Men out of their Mistakes, who have no settled Notions, as to dispossess a Vagrant of his Habitation, who has no settled abode' (III. X. 4. 21–25.: 492). When Locke extends this to philosophical discourse we find him remarking that it is plain in common discourse that the meaning of the terms 'body' and 'extension' are distinct from one another, yet there are those 'who find it necessary to confound their signification' (III. X. 6. 33–4.: 493). He is clearly talking about Descartes and the Cartesians.

Questions

15. What are the two kinds of public discourse that Locke identifies? Against which of these do we measure the perfection or imperfection of words?
16. When Locke says that each of the various ideas of gold that people put together is just as good as the next, has he forgotten that one such idea might be demonstrated to be more adequate than another?
17. Locke claims that the Bible and other such revelations are ambiguous because of the numerous ancient modal notions in them. He goes on to claim that the teleological argument for the existence of God and other related proofs do much better at establishing God's existence and the obedience due to him. Do you agree with him? Why or why not?
18. What is the difference between imperfections and abuses of language?
19. What is the abuse of language that Locke thinks the Cartesians commit in conflating the terms 'body' and 'extension'?

Remedies for imperfections and abuses

The remedies for the inconveniences and abuses of language that Locke offers in chapter XI of Book III follow naturally from the nature of those inconveniences and abuses. He notes that reforming language is a pretty hopeless enterprise and that those who love controversy will hardly be interested in having their disagreements curtailed, so his efforts at reform are addressed to those who pretend seriously to search after or maintain the truth. He claims that they should think themselves obliged to study how they might deliver themselves without the obscurity, doubtfulness or equivocation to which words are naturally liable (III. XI. 3. 25–29.: 509).

Locke then offers a series of rules that build on one another. The first is that words need to mean something. So, don't use words without meaning. As noted above, Locke thinks there are people who violate this rule both in civil and in philosophical discourse (III. XI. 8. 16–31.: 512). The second rule is that it is not enough to have some ideas to provide the meaning for words; if they are simple they should be clear and distinct and if they are complex they should be determinate, that is one should know what all of the ideas in the complex are. This is important for modal words and especially for moral terms, as these have no settled object in nature from which the ideas are taken (III. XI. 9. 32–28.: 512–13).

Here Locke introduces a procedure that is a bit like Descartes' method of analysis or Hume's microscope. In Hume's case the procedure is to take a complex idea and trace all of its simple ideas back to the impression from which they derive. Locke wants us to be able to reduce a complex idea such as justice into its component parts. If one of the parts is not clear and distinct, then the whole complex will be confused. Locke expects that many people will reject this requirement as too difficult, but he claims that unless it is done it will be a source of confusion and obscurity in one's own thinking and wrangling with others.

In respect of the names of substances, one must go beyond the requirement that one should have determinate ideas and that one must be sure that '*Names must also be comfortable to Things*, as they exist' (III. XI. 10. 31.: 513). Presumably 'conformable' here means just what it did in II.XXX where he defines the term as either things causing or being patterns for (resembling) ideas. Thus such ideas will be real rather than fantastical. Locke remarks that it would be good if this were extended to common conversation and the ordinary affairs of life, but then turns this reflection around, remarking: 'Vulgar notions suit Vulgar Discourses, and both, though confused enough, yet serve pretty well the Market, and the Wake. Merchants and Lovers, Cooks and Taylors, have Words wherewithal to dispatch their ordinary Affairs; and so, I think, might Philosophers and Disputants too, if they had a Mind to Understand, and to be clearly Understood' (III. XI. 10. 6–9.: 514). So, we are back to the original point that it is particularly in philosophical discourse that these rules need to be followed, at least by those who are seriously pursuing the truth.

The third rule is that one should follow common usage in applying words to ideas. Locke remarks that: 'Words, especially of languages already framed, being no Man's private possession, but the common measure of Commerce and Communication, 'tis not for anyone, at pleasure, to change the Stamp they are current in' (III. XI. 11. 13–16.: 514). The next rule is that where common usage fails for one reason or another, he who introduces a new word, or uses an old one in a new way, or where common usage is insufficiently precise, must declare what the meaning of the word is (III. XI. 12. 34–13.: 514–5).

Locke next turns to definitions and picks up the point he made in chapter III of Book III that simple ideas are not subject to definition, while mixed modes are subject to definition and substances are in some ways subject to definition and in others not (III. XI. 13. 14–21.: 515). Because simple ideas are not capable of definition, we either have to display their meaning to those who do not understand by talking about some subject in which one finds that quality, or by ostension, that is by actually pointing out some instance of that quality.

It is in respect of the difference between morality and natural philosophy that the difference between modes and substances displays its importance for Locke. Because moral terms are mixed modes, they are all capable of precise definition, and Locke claims that, because they are capable of precise definition, morality is as capable of demonstration as mathematics. Natural philosophy, by contrast, is concerned with substances and so such discourse is rarely if ever going to reach the level of demonstration. In substances, both showing and defining may well be necessary.

Beyond this, since our ideas of substances are supposed to correspond to the nature of things, we cannot rest with common usage but must enquire into the natural history of that sort of thing in order to make our ideas conform with reality. One useful way of proceeding would be for those engaged in this kind of enquiry to list all of the simple ideas that they find in a particular sort of substance. This would eliminate much of the ambiguity attendant on people using different lists of greater and lesser length. Locke suggests that producing a dictionary would be of great use, but remarks that it is probably impractical (III. XI. 25. 7–10.: 522). Similarly, he argues that as pictures often serve better to inform one of what plant or animal a word stands for than do lengthy definitions, this is also true of artefacts and clothing.

The fifth rule is to avoid equivocation: one should use the same word in the same way. There are so many things in the world that we are likely to end up using the same word for more than one of them. Usually readers can follow a change in meaning, but where this is not the case, it is the obligation of the writer to provide a sufficient guide (III. IX. 26. 23–34.: 523).

Questions

20. Why does Locke think that reforming language is a project that is not very likely to succeed? To whom are Locke's efforts at reforming language addressed?
21. How do Locke's proposed rules relate to his distinctions between simple ideas, simple and mixed modes and substances?

BOOK IV OF THE ESSAY

Knowledge

In the fourth book of *An Essay Concerning Human Understanding*, Locke tells us what knowledge is and what humans can know and what they cannot (not simply what they do and do not happen to know). Locke defines knowledge as 'the perception of the connexion and agreement or disagreement and repugnancy of any of our Ideas' (IV. I. 1.: 525). This definition of knowledge contrasts with the Cartesian definition of certain knowledge in Meditation III: ' ... whatever I conceive very clearly and distinctly is true' (Descartes: 87). Locke's account of knowledge allows him to say that we can know substances in spite of the fact that our ideas of them always include the obscure and relative idea of substance in general. Still, Locke's definition of knowledge raises a problem analogous to those we have seen with perception and language. If knowledge is the perception of the agreement or disagreement of any of our ideas, are we not trapped in the circle of our own ideas? What about knowing the real existence of things? Locke is plainly aware of this problem and addresses it at several points in Book IV, most notably in chapters IV and V.

We might wonder how Locke's account of knowledge compares with that offered in contemporary philosophy. Is it, for example, a version of the justified true belief account of knowledge? On this account X knows that P (where X is a person and P is a proposition) if and only if: 1. P is true; 2. X believes that P; and 3. X is justified in believing that P. The answer is that Locke's account of knowledge does require that what is known be true and believed, but Locke's account of justification requires certainty, while the account of justification offered by most proponents of the justified true belief account today is significantly weaker and consequently would allow much of what Locke calls probability to count as knowledge. Still, Locke is not simply trying to give the necessary and sufficient conditions for knowledge. Rather, in addition to defining knowledge, he is trying to determine what abilities and powers we have or lack, along with the way the universe is, that make knowledge possible in some cases and impossible in others. This is a deeper and more interesting enquiry than the one aiming only at the definition of knowledge.

Kinds of agreement and disagreement of ideas

Having defined knowledge in the first part of chapter I of Book IV, Locke then enumerates the kinds of agreement or disagreement of ideas and then the 'several ways wherein the Mind is possessed of Truth, each of which is called *Knowledge* (IV. I. 8. 30–31.: 527). The four kinds of agreement and disagreement are: 1. Identity and Diversity; 2. Relation; 3. Co-existence or necessary connexion; and 4. Real existence. Locke claims that the ability of the mind to determine that its ideas are identical with themselves and different from others is absolutely fundamental. Without this ability there would be 'no Knowledge, no Reasoning, no Imagination, no distinct Thoughts at all' (IV. I. 4. 4–5.: 526). Locke claims that though this ability can be given – general formulations such as the reflexive character of identity or the law of non-contradiction – these formulations are simply generalizations from the ability of the mind to distinguish particular ideas such as white from black. We should note that he has already been concerned with this topic in Book I where he argues that these maxims are not innate and gives the positive account that he is repeating here. This is Locke's first salvo in Book IV against the maxims of the scholastics. He takes these up specifically in Book IV, chapter VII.

Relation is the '*Perception of the Relation between any two Ideas*, of what kind soever, whether Substances, Modes or any other' (IV. I. 5. 28–29.: 526). What Locke has in mind here is the next step beyond being able to see that one particular idea is identical with itself and different from others. Now we are comparing ideas to see the ways in which they agree and disagree. Once again, Locke claims that without this ability we could have no knowledge at all. Given his definition of knowledge this is clearly correct.

The third kind of agreement or disagreement is co-existence or necessary connection of properties in a single subject. This kind of knowledge relates chiefly to substances and the question is what ideas are always in the particular set that determines the nominal essence. Locke gives the example of gold, where fixedness (the power to remain unconsumed in fire) 'always accompanies, and is join'd with that particular sort of Yellowness, Weight, Fusibility, Malleableness and Solubility in *Aqua Regia*, which make our complex Idea, signified by the word *Gold*' (IV. I. 6. 5–8.: 527). Presumably perceiving this kind of agreement and disagreement of ideas gives us the knowledge of nominal essences of substances.

Finally, in section 7, he mentions a fourth kind of knowledge. This is the knowledge of actual real existence agreeing with any idea. Presumably if we were to adopt Hume's distinction between impressions and ideas, the question would be how do we know that impressions come from and correspond with objects outside us? Locke returns to this topic in chapter II, section 14 and then again in chapter XI.

Turning to the several ways in which the mind possesses truth, Locke distinguishes between actual and habitual knowledge. Actual knowledge is that state in which the mind views the agreements or disagreements of its ideas or their relations to one another. Habitual knowledge, by contrast, is that in which a man has seen the agreement or disagreement of the ideas in which a proposition consists, so that whenever he remembers it he 'without doubt or hesitation, embraces the right side, assents to or is certain of the Truth of it' (IV. I. 8. 2–4.: 528). There are, Locke says, vulgarly speaking, two degrees of habitual knowledge. The first is where the agreements and disagreements of ideas are preserved in memory. This, Locke claims, is true of all our intuitive knowledge. The second degree has to do with demonstrative knowledge. In this second case one was convinced of the truth of a proposition by a proof, and one now retains the conviction of truth without the proof. Upon reflection, Locke thinks that this should still count as knowledge.

Questions

1. What is Locke's account of knowledge and in what ways is it similar to and different from the justified true belief account of knowledge?
2. What are the four kinds of agreement or disagreement of ideas and how do they relate to Locke's account of knowledge?

3.   What is the difference between actual and habitual knowledge for Locke?

Intuitive, demonstrative and sensible evidence

In Chapter II Locke gives us an account of intuitive, demonstrative and sensitive knowledge. These different kinds of knowledge result from the mind having different ways of perceiving the agreement or disagreement of ideas. These different ways of perceiving provide different degrees of evidence. Intuitive knowledge involves the mind perceiving 'the Agreement or Disagreement of two *Ideas* immediately by themselves, without the intervention of any other' (IV. II. 1. 29–1.: 530–1). In this case, Locke tells us, the mind perceives truth effortlessly just as the eye perceives light. This kind of knowledge 'is the clearest and most certain, that humane Frailty is capable of' (IV. II. 1. 9–10.: 531).

Demonstrative knowledge is the second degree of certainty. It depends on intuitive knowledge for its efficacy. In this case, one looks at two ideas and cannot immediately see the agreements and disagreements between them. The remedy for this is to find other ideas that connect the two and display their agreements or disagreements. For each intermediary idea, however, there have to be intuitive connections either with the original ideas or with the neighbouring links in the chain of ideas. The search for such intermediate ideas is called *reasoning*. The chain of ideas that demonstrates the agreement or disagreement of two ideas is a *proof* and where the proof of the agreement or disagreement 'is plainly clearly perceived, it is called *Demonstration*' (IV. II. 3. 20–21.: 532). This kind of knowledge is of the second degree, because it is '*not* altogether so clear and bright, nor the assent so ready, as in intuitive knowledge' (IV. II. 4. 26–27.: 532). Demonstrative knowledge requires work, a steady application and pursuit, pains and attention. Another difference is that before one acquires demonstrative knowledge there is doubt, where this is not so with intuitive knowledge. Additionally, long proofs are subject to mistake and error in a way that is not true of intuitive knowledge.

At IV. II. 8.: 534 in his next remark about Maxims, Locke says that the mistaken claim that all reasoning is from principles already known very likely derives from the necessity of having intuitive knowledge of the connection between each step and the next in a proof. Again he refers us to his discussion of propositions and maxims in IV. VII.

Locke also remarks that it is often thought that mathematics alone is capable of demonstrative certainty. He thinks that this is not so. Locke claims that 'where it can perceive the agreement of any two Ideas, by an intuitive perception of the agreement or disagreement they have with any intermediate *Ideas*, there the Mind is capable of Demonstration, which is not limited to Ideas of Extension, Figure and Number and their Modes' (IV. II. 9. 1–5.: 535). This kind of reasoning is, for example, more difficult with colours, but where colours are clear and distinct from one another we can produce demonstrations about them. This is also true of other secondary qualities and their modes (IV. II. 13. 30–35.: 536).

In section 14 Locke returns to the issue of sensitive knowledge that he raised in section 7 of Book IV, chapter I. Locke raises the question at IV. II. 14. 9–14.: 537). It is intuitively clear that we have the idea, but how can we infer from this that there is an object corresponding to it since it is sometimes the case that: 'Men may have such *Ideas* in their Minds, when no such Thing exists, no such Object affects their Senses'. In answer, Locke makes what amounts to Hume's distinction between ideas and impressions, arguing that there is as great a difference between the idea of the sun perceived during the day and remembered during the night, wormwood tasted during the day and later remembered, and so forth, as there is 'between any two distinct Ideas' (IV. II. 14. 22.: 537).

Locke then proceeds to take up Descartes' dream hypothesis which is, in effect, simply our having an intuitively clear idea without there being an object external to us causing that idea. Locke makes several points in response. The first is that in dreams, reasoning and argument are of no use, and thus truth and knowledge are nothing. This seems to be largely correct. Second, he points out that there is another clear difference between dreaming and waking. When you find yourself in your waking state in a fire you are likely to get painfully burned. If you dream that you are in a fire you are not going to get the same sensation of pain. This is a perceptive point. Locke goes on to remark that if the sceptic is resolved to maintain that there is no difference, that even the intense sensation of pain that we normally associate with being burned in a waking state is really a dream, then, in effect, there is no difference between dreaming and waking that is of any importance to us. Here one might compare the answer that Locke gives with that of the Wittgensteinian philosopher O.K. Bouwsma in 'Descartes'

Skepticism of the Senses' or Bouwsma's similar argument in 'Descartes' Evil Genius'. Locke concludes that we can add sensitive knowledge to the category of things that we know.

Finally Locke asks whether if the ideas whose agreement or disagreement we perceive are obscure, wouldn't this make our knowledge correspondingly obscure? Were this so, Locke's account of knowledge would be identical to that of Descartes. Locke, unsurprisingly, claims that this is not the case. He claims, in effect, that clearness and distinctness of ideas is a necessary but not a sufficient condition for knowledge, because if the ideas are confused then the mind cannot perceive clearly. But it is possible that the ideas are clear and distinct, but there is not a clear and distinct perception.

Questions

4. What is intuitive knowledge?
5. What is demonstrative knowledge? How does intuitive knowledge relate to demonstrative knowledge?
6. Why does Locke claim that it is not mathematics alone that is capable of demonstration?
7. What is sensitive knowledge?
8. In defending the claim that there is sensitive knowledge, Locke rejects Descartes' dream hypothesis. Why would the dream hypothesis threaten sensitive knowledge and why does Locke reject it?
9. If Locke does not take sceptical arguments seriously, why then is sensitive knowledge so limited?
10. Is Locke conceding too much to the Cartesians in allowing clear and distinct ideas to be a necessary condition for knowledge? What, on his account, does this do to knowledge of substances?

The extent of our knowledge

In some ways the discussion of the extent of human knowledge is the culmination of the entire project of *An Essay Concerning Human Understanding*. From his definition of knowledge and the discussion of kinds and degrees of knowledge, Locke makes a series of points about the extent of human knowledge. First, since knowledge is the perception of the agreement or disagreement of ideas, 'we can have *Knowledge* no farther than we have *Ideas*' (IV. III. 1. 28.: 538). The perception of the agreement of ideas depends either on intuition, demonstration or sensation so we cannot have intuitive or demonstrative knowledge that extends itself to all our ideas. Sensitive knowledge 'reaching no farther than the Existence of Things actually present to our senses, is yet much narrower than either of the former' (IV. III. 5. 28–30.: 539). From all this, it follows that the extent of our knowledge neither reaches to 'the Reality of Things' or even the extent of our own ideas (IV. III. 6. 32–33.: 539). Other creatures, perhaps angels, may have much more expansive knowledge than we do, limited as we are to our few and not very acute senses. Still, Locke claims, we would be in great shape if our knowledge were to reach as far as our ideas, and if we had few doubts and not much thinking to engage in about the ideas we have. But this is not our situation. Still, Locke insists, human knowledge can be greatly improved. This could be done if men would 'sincerely, and with Freedom of Mind, employ all the Industry and Labour of Thought, in improving the means of discovering the Truth, which they do for the colouring or support of Falsehood, to maintain a System, Interest or Party, they are once engaged in' (IV. III. 6.11–15.: 540). Locke then returns to the theme that we are probably not going to resolve some issues about the ideas that we do have (IV. IV. 6. 15–19.: 540).

The first example he gives is the mathematical problem of squaring the circle. This is a really bad example, because mathematicians had already concluded that it was impossible to do this. Thus, this is one of those questions where Locke's project of defining the limits of human knowledge to end disagreement worked, but Locke did not know this. If a sceptic were to say, you will never know if there is a circle with the same area as this square, the proper answer would be 'You are quite right. Let's talk about something we can know'.

The second example is that of thinking matter. Locke claims that while we have the ideas of 'thinking' and 'matter', we shall perhaps never be able to know whether God has 'not given to some Systems of Matter, fitly disposed, a power to perceive and think, or else joined and fixed to Matter, so disposed, a thinking, immaterial substance' (IV. III. 6. 26–1.: 540–1). Locke goes on to claim that it is just as hard to conceive the one possibility as the other, and that while he can see a contradiction in God being material, he can see no contradiction in an immaterial God superadding the power of thinking to matter. This example struck the eighteenth century like a bombshell and was hotly debated for roughly the next hundred years. There are a number of good accounts of these controversies, including those of Yolton (1983), Fox and Martin and Barresi.

The implication of Locke's agnosticism about whether matter can think is that there is no proof of the immateriality of the soul. Locke is quite unperturbed about this. He claims that 'All the great Ends of Morality and Religion, are well enough secured, without philosophical Proofs of the Soul's Immateriality' (IV. III. 6. 6–8.: 542). This doctrine is not needed to explain the Resurrection of the Dead and the punishments and rewards that will follow. So, there is no great necessity to determine the issue one way or the other. There is thus a connection here with Locke's account of personal identity in II. XXVII. There Locke claims that it does not matter what kinds of substances compose persons, whether simple or compounded, material or immaterial.

Returning to the issue of the extent of our knowledge in IV. III. 7., Locke takes up the four kinds of agreement and disagreement of ideas he had identified in IV. I. Here we get a more detailed account of what we do and do not know. As for identity, Locke claims that we have intuitive knowledge that all of our ideas are identical with themselves and different from all others. So, our knowledge of identity is as wide as our ideas. This seems to leave out cases of informative identities. I may have an idea of Cicero and an idea of Tully, but not know that Cicero is Tully. When I discover that Cicero is Tully then I am learning something I didn't know before. Locke's response to this might have been that such informative identities require some form of demonstration and so should not be listed here. In fact, Locke is going to tell us later (at IV. VIII. 3. 3–8) that he does not believe in informative identity statements.

In respect of our knowledge of the agreement and disagreement of ideas concerning the co-existence of properties, it turns out that we know very little. Locke remarks that while our knowledge here is 'short', yet it 'consists of the greatest and most material part of our Knowledge concerning Substances' (IV. III. 9. 6–7.: 544). Our ideas of species are collections of ideas that go together and when we want to know more about a substance we are again asking what properties co-exist in that substance.

There are reasons why our knowledge of the co-existence of

properties is so limited. Unfortunately, our ideas of properties for the most part have no visible necessary connection with one another. Second, because most of the ideas of properties are ideas of secondary qualities which 'depending all (as has been shewn) upon the Primary qualities of their minute and insensible parts, or if not upon them, upon something yet more remote from our Comprehension, 'tis impossible that we should know, which have a necessary union or inconsistency one with another' (IV. III. 11. 29–33.: 544). This particular formulation is interesting, because Locke is allowing that there may be 'something yet more remote from our Comprehension' that is responsible for our experience of substances. Given the advances in physics over the next 300 years, this formulation seems to be the most prescient Locke gives. Finally, there is no discoverable connection between the ideas of secondary qualities and the primary qualities that cause them.

In the case of primary qualities, we can conceive how 'the size, figure and motion of one Body should cause a change in the size, figure and motion of another body' (IV. III. 13. 16–17.: 545). The separation of parts of one body upon the intrusion of another and the change from rest to motion upon impact seem to have some connection with one another. And if we knew more about particles there is likely much more that we could discover. But this is not the case with the connection between primary and secondary qualities. Locke goes on to say that we are so far from knowing what particular combination of figure, size and motion of parts 'produce in us a Yellow Colour, a sweet Taste or a sharp Sound, that we can by no means conceive how any *size, figure* or *motion* of Particles, can possibly produce in us the *Idea* of any *Colour, Taste* or *Sound* whatsoever; there is no conceivable *connexion* betwixt the one and the other' (IV. III. 13. 30–34.: 545). Locke is here enunciating one of the problems that dualists and neo-dualists have asserted is an insuperable bar to a materialist account of mind. This is sometimes called the problem of *qualia* or subjective human experience. So, in respect of the co-existence of properties our knowledge reaches only a little farther than our experience. Experience is always of particulars. If we are going to generalize beyond our experience, we need to grasp the necessary connections between properties and, for all the reasons given above, Locke thinks we are not going to get very far with this.

In section 15 of Book IV, chapter III, Locke turns to the

'*incompatibility or repugnancy to co-existence*'. This means he wants
to know which ideas cannot co-exist together. Here he notes that we
may know that each subject of a primary quality may have only one
particular determinate of that quality at a time. So, this wall has a
particular height, e.g. six feet, at a particular place, at a particular
time and cannot have some other height at the same place and at
the same time. The same is true of each secondary quality.

In section 16 he takes up the powers of substances to change the
sensible qualities of other bodies (the tertiary qualities). Again
Locke claims that our knowledge in this case does not reach much
beyond our experience. The problem is much the same. We don't
know the texture and motion of parts upon which the active and
passive powers of substances depend. Nor are we likely to be able to
discover them. Here Locke remarks that the corpuscularian hypothesis is the one which is thought to go the farthest in giving an
intelligible explanation of the qualities of bodies. But whether this is
so or not, whatever hypothesis we adopt, we are not likely to get
very far in advancing our knowledge of corporeal substances until
we can determine which qualities of bodies are necessarily connected with one another and which are incompatible. In this particular area we must depend on experience and we see by the work
of some accomplished men that it can be improved, though others
(and here Locke mentions the alchemists) have not done so.

If we are in the dark about the powers and operations of bodies,
it is clear that we are much more so about spirits. Here we have no
ideas except those we have of ourselves. Consequently, all we can
do, in this case, is use ourselves as an analogy and imagine a progression of spirits up to God (III. VI. 11.: 445–6 and IV. III. 27.:
557–8).

Locke now turns to the third sort of agreement or disagreement
of ideas, that of relations other than co-existence. This is the largest
field of our knowledge and so the most difficult to determine how
far it extends. The problem is that we just don't know where human
ingenuity will be able to find intermediate ideas that will connect
two remote ideas. Locke remarks that those who are ignorant of
algebra cannot imagine the wonders it can accomplish in this regard. He also thinks it possible that demonstrations can be given in
other areas besides mathematics. Here Locke makes the suggestion
that having clear ideas of God and ourselves we might be able to
use these as 'Foundations of our Duty and Rules of Action, as

might place *Morality among the Sciences Capable of Demonstration*' (IV. III. 18. 16–17.: 549). There are other similar propositions about justice and government that Locke thinks can be demonstrated. In the next two sections (18–20) Locke goes on to explain why he thinks quantity has been taken to be more capable of demonstration than morality or other things. In section 21 of Book IV, chapter III, Locke turns to the fourth kind of knowledge, that of the real, actual existence of things.

In respect of our knowledge of real existence, Locke claims that 'we have an intuitive knowledge of our own Existence; a demonstrative knowledge of the Existence of God; of the Existence of any thing else, we have no other but a sensitive Knowledge, which extends not beyond the Objects present to our Senses' (IV. III. 21. 36–4.: 552–3). The first two are strikingly similar to conclusions Descartes came to in the *Meditations* (Descartes: 73–159). The differences are also illuminating. Descartes starts from the claim of knowing his own existence to a claim of knowing that his essence is to be a thinking thing in a similar way. Locke rejects the Cartesian claim to be a thinking thing for excellent reasons. Similarly, while both hold that our knowledge of bodies is limited, Descartes thinks we have innate knowledge of the essence of bodies and that we can have clear and distinct ideas of them insofar as they can be modeled by mathematics. The existence of material bodies is much more problematic and our knowledge of this ultimately depends on God's benevolence in not deceiving us. Locke's account of sensitive knowledge involves a firm rejection of scepticism in contrast with the Cartesian acceptance of the coherence of the Dream and Evil Demon hypotheses.

In sections 22–30 Locke turns to the dark side and an account of our ignorance. It is unnecessary to treat this in any great detail; in explaining our knowledge and its extent, Locke has perforce already listed virtually all the factors that cause our ignorance. It is, however, worth noting that to make clear the extent of our ignorance Locke displays what he regards as the vast extent and grandeur of the universe in which we inhabit such a tiny place.

In section 31 he announces that he is now going to consider a different parameter measuring the extent of our knowledge, namely universality. It turns out that things are universal only insofar as they are abstract. So, we know essences only by contemplating our own abstract ideas. Existence, on the other hand, is known by experience.

Questions

11. How does the extent of ideas place a limit on human knowledge?
12. Why does making the distinction between the degrees of knowledge, intuitive, demonstrative and sensitive, still further narrow the reach of human knowledge beyond the limit placed by the extent of ideas?
13. In IV. III. 6 Locke gives examples of issues about our own ideas that we will very likely not be able to resolve. What are these?
14. Do you agree with Locke that the hypothesis that matter can think is just as plausible as the one that God can connect an immaterial soul to a body?
15. In IV. III. 7. Locke returns to the four kinds of agreement or disagreement he identified in IV I. He now gives us a more detailed account of what we can and cannot know. So, what does he think we can and cannot know?
16. Does Locke think the problem that we cannot conceive of how primary qualities cause particular subjective experiences in us is a bar to a materialist account of mind, or does he think it applies to all theories, materialist and dualist alike?
17. Clearly Locke was much too pessimistic about our knowledge of the co-existence of properties and powers of material substances. Where was Locke correct and where did he go wrong?

The reality of knowledge

In Book IV, chapter IV, Locke takes up the issue of the relation of ideas to reality. Since he has defined knowledge as the perception of the agreement or disagreement of our ideas, the relation of ideas to reality becomes crucially important. For, if our ideas have nothing to do with reality, then as Locke says: ' 'Tis no matter how things are: so a man observe but the agreement of his own Imaginations, and talk conformably, it is all Truth, all Certainty. Such Castles in the Air will be such strong Holds of Truth, as the Demonstrations of Euclid' (IV. IV. 1. 4–8.: 563). Another way to put the problem is that Locke seems to have a coherence theory of knowledge. But what is needed is not just coherence, but correspondence. Where is the correspondence?

In section 2 Locke accepts the problem as genuine. In section 3 he restates it. The mind doesn't know things immediately but only by the intervention of ideas. Our knowledge is only real insofar as 'there is a conformity between our *Ideas* and the Reality of Things. But what shall be here the Criterion? How shall the mind, when it perceives nothing but its own *Ideas*, know that they agree with Things themselves?' (IV. IV. 3. 29–32.: 563). Locke thus sees that he has the same problem as the one he complained about in Malebranche, but presumably, as J.L. Mackie remarked, Locke thinks he has the resources to solve that problem. So, what ideas can we know conform to reality?

First, Locke tells us that there are simple ideas that we ourselves cannot make. These are the 'natural and regular Productions of things without us, really operating upon us; and so carry with them all the conformity which is intended, or which our state requires' (IV. IV. 4. 5–7.: 564). Locke is using the term 'conformity' much as he did in the discussion of the real versus fantastical ideas in Book II, chapter XXX. So ideas of secondary qualities conform to reality as much as the ideas of primary qualities do, though the primary qualities resemble the things that cause them while the secondary qualities do not. And Locke says 'this conformity between our simple *Ideas* and the existence of Things, is sufficient for real Knowledge' (IV. IV. 4. 15–16.: 564).

The second class of ideas that we can be sure conform to reality are all our complex ideas except those of substances. These are ideas of modes. Since these ideas are not intended to copy any thing, 'not referred to the existence of any thing, as to their Originals, *cannot want any conformity necessary to real Knowledge*' (IV. IV. 5. 19–20.: 564). Since things conform to these ideas, rather than the ideas representing things, in this case 'we cannot miss of an undoubted reality' (IV. IV. 5. 34–35.: 564).

The first example of such modal ideas is mathematics. Locke claims that in this case we do not doubt that we have real knowledge about ideas that may be only in our minds. Insofar as real existing things agree with these ideas, we may have true knowledge of them as well. Our moral knowledge is also capable of being real knowledge for analogous reasons. Locke had previously made this point in III. XI. 16.

The reader may be inclined to object that all this discussion of modes has largely avoided the question of the real existence of objects. Locke makes this objection for the reader at IV. IV. 8. His reply is that the reason that he seems to pay so little heed to the real existence of things is that 'most of those Discourses, which take up the Thoughts and engage the Disputes of those who pretend to make it their Business to enquire after Truth and Certainty, will I presume, upon examination be found to be *general propositions*, and Notions in which existence is not concerned' (IV. IV. 8. 3–7.: 566). He again makes the point that things and people have to agree to mathematical and moral ideas, not the other way round. Locke raises yet another objection, namely that if moral ideas are simply modes, then anyone can make up whatever ideas they want and thus 'What Strange Notions there will be of *Justice* and *Temperance?* What confusion of Vertues and Vices, if every one may make what *Ideas* of them he pleases?' (IV. IV. 9. 27–29.: 566). Locke claims that this will simply amount to misnaming, and that when we see what ideas the names stand for, the demonstrations of the properties that follow will sort themselves out in both mathematics and morality.

In section 10, Locke turns to our ideas of substances. Here Locke admits that since these ideas are referred to external archetypes or external patterns and may differ from those archetypes by having more or different ideas than are united in them, some of our ideas of substances may not be real. 'Real', as Locke is using it here, fits his official definition in II. XXX, that is, conforming to reality. 'Conforming' implies regular causation, but not necessarily resemblance. In the construction of mixed modes all that is really required is coherence or consistency. But here we need correspondence with the real pattern of qualities as well. Our knowledge does not reach very far because we don't know the real essences of substances that are the cause of the strict union of qualities in those substances. Without this we are limited to what we learn from experience. To make our knowledge of substances real, 'our *Ideas* must be taken from the real existence of things. Whatever simple ideas have been found to co-exist in any Substance, these we may with confidence join together again, and so make abstract *Ideas* of Substances. For whatever have once had a union in Nature, may be united again' (IV. IV. 12. 3–7.: 569).

In the remainder of this chapter (sections 13 through 18) Locke is defending his claim (developed in Book III) that the abstract ideas that we make of particular kinds of substances are the species or nominal essences of those kinds. Locke claims that in adopting his view 'we should think about things with greater freedom and perhaps less confusion than we do' (IV. IV. 13. 11–12.: 569). The position that Locke is rejecting is Aristotelian essentialism, and particularly that names are determined by real essences that have determinate boundaries and 'wherein all the things of the same denomination did exactly and equally partake' (IV. IV. 13. 3–7.: 569). To show the inadequacy of this position, Locke wants to consider a changeling. He defines a changeling as 'the Idea of Shape, Motion and Life of a Man without Reason' (IV. IV. 13. 24–25.: 569). He asks rhetorically whether a changeling, that is a man without reason, is not a new species, one that would be as distinct from the already existing species of 'man' and 'beast' as the idea of 'an ass with reason' would be. And if asked what are these things between man and beast, Locke would answer changelings! If it were then asked if this is a different species, what will become of them in the next life, Locke's response is first that this is God's business to determine and not his; second, that the force of the question is built on one or another of two false suppositions. The first is that a human shape guarantees immortality. Shape is surely not the determinant of immortality! This would altogether leave out the soul or spirit. The reply to this is that shape does not make one immortal, rather it 'is the sign of a rational Soul within, that is immortal' (IV. IV. 15. 19.: 571). Locke's response to this is that he wants to know who made it so, for just saying it will not make it so. Locke then offers some counter-examples to this second false assumption. It would follow, if having a human shape is the sign of a rational soul within, that either a dead man or a sculpture having a human form should have a rational soul. The claim that a human shape is the sign of a rational soul makes even less sense when one considers that a changeling, while it has the shape of a man, displays less reason in its actions than do those of some beasts.

Locke next considers the objection that the changeling is the child of rational parents and should therefore be considered as having a rational soul. But if this were so, Locke argues, no one would dare to destroy 'ill-formed and misshaped productions' (IV. IV. 16. 34.: 571). But, Locke's opponents respond, these are monsters. Locke proceeds to compare changelings with monsters. The first has a defective mind (it lacks reason) while the second has a defective body. So, Locke asks, will a defect in a body determine that something is not human while a defect in the mind, the far more noble and perhaps essential part, will not? This would again make shape the measure of man. Clearly Locke has already rejected the notion that shape alone should determine whether something is human. Locke thinks that people actually do think this way while at the same time disowning their opinion. Locke starts with the claim that the well-shaped changeling has a rational soul, though it appears not to. Now start changing the shape. 'Make the Ears a little longer and more pointed, and the Nose a little flatter than ordinary, and then you begin to Boggle' (IV. IV. 16. 13–16.: 572). Continuing the process of altering the face, making it less and less human and more and more animal-like, an opponent will conclude that it is a monster. Since it is a monster, the opponent will conclude that it does not have a rational soul and so must be destroyed. But, what is the criterion for determining that a being with such a shape has a rational soul while the one next to it does not? 'For 'till that be done', Locke says, 'we talk at random of Man: and shall always, I fear, do so, as long as we give up to certain Sounds, and the Imagination of settled and fixed species in Nature, we know not what' (IV. IV. 16. 31–34.: 572). Locke goes on to remark that those who argue that a misshapen foetus is a monster, in fact are doing just what they are arguing against: making a new species between man and beast. This shows that one should give up the Aristotelian/ scholastic doctrine of a fixed number of natural kinds.

This example is of some importance, because scholars have proposed that Locke's nominal essence theory, and in particular his account of man, has certain problems. In particular, it opens the possibility that racists, for example, might define 'human being' as they please. Professor Harry Bracken, for example, has made just such a charge (Bracken, 1973). But the result of the arguments in sections 13–18 is that it is the acceptance of the Aristotelian/ scholastic doctrine of fixed species, a doctrine that cannot deal with intermediate forms and borderline cases, that leads us to talk inconsistently or, as Locke says, 'at random' of man. Locke thinks that his own procedure of allowing for the creation of intermediate species will allow us to argue about what should go into our account of man and thus avoid these inconsistencies and the inability to produce criteria to distinguish one species from another. We will see more of this when we reach Book IV, chapter VII, 'Of Maxims'.

Questions

18. What is the problem of the reality of knowledge? How does it parallel the problems raised about ideas and perception, and ideas and language, in Books II and III respectively?
19. What is Locke's response to the problem?
20. Locke claims that although moral ideas are modes, and thus different people can put together their own moral ideas, this is no real problem. This is because what they are doing is simply misnaming, like calling a square a triangle. Is this claim plausible?
21. Why is the problem of the reality of knowledge more difficult in the case of substances than with mixed modes?

Truth and generality

In chapter V, Locke discusses the nature of truth. He defines truth as '*the joining or separating of Signs, as the things signified by them do agree or disagree one with another*' (IV. V. 2. 7–9.: 575). The joining and separating here is the making of propositions and so strictly speaking truth belongs only to propositions. There are mental and verbal propositions and so the corresponding two sorts of truth. Locke goes on to discuss the relation between these two sorts of proposition and why it is difficult to deal with them separately. These propositions affirm or deny the agreement or disagreement of ideas or words, and insofar as they do this correctly or incorrectly are either true or false. If the proposition is of ideas, then this is a mental truth; if of words, then a verbal one. Locke makes some further distinctions between purely verbal and trifling truths and real and instructive truths. The latter are the object of real knowledge.

In IV. V. 7, Locke returns to the vital issues raised in the previous chapter about real knowledge. He remarks that the same doubt that occurred about knowledge is likely to occur here about truth. If truth is as Locke has defined it, then '*the Knowledge of Truth is not so valuable a Thing* as it is taken to be; nor worth the Pains and

Time Men imploy in the search of it: since, *by this account*, it amount to no more than the Conformity of Words, to the *Chimeras* of Men's Brains' (IV. V. 7. 5–8.: 577). If all we have here is the consistency of ideas, it will be as much true that a centaur is an animal as that a man is an animal. Locke says that he might give the same answer to this problem of distinguishing real from chimerical truth as he did in the previous chapter to distinguish real and imaginary knowledge, but he goes on to make a distinction between verbal and real truths. Our words derive meaning only from our ideas, but since they also refer to things, truth is merely verbal 'when they stand for Ideas in the Mind, that have not an agreement with the Reality of Things' (IV. V. 7. 33–4.: 577). As a consequence, both truth and knowledge can be separated into verbal and real. Verbal truth has only to do with the agreement or disagreement of our ideas, while for real truth we not only have agreement of ideas but the 'Capacity of having an Existence in Nature' (IV. V. 7. 2.: 578). So real truth requires correspondence (or at least the capacity for correspondence) as well as consistency of ideas. How should we think of this correspondence? It might be either in terms of Hume's distinction between ideas and impressions (a distinction that Locke makes but does not name) or between impressions and things. Locke's language in the passage just quoted might well suggest the ideas/impression distinction, since he talks about our ideas having the capacity of existing in nature. On the other hand, this may be yet another case where what Locke means (though he doesn't say it clearly) is that our ideas must correspond (or conform or agree to use Lockean terms) to qualities capable of having an existence in nature. In either case, we again have a clear difference between Locke's representative realism and that of Malebranche, discussed earlier in the section on Resemblance and representative theories of perception in Book II. It is the causal element in Locke's theory that allows him to distinguish between a horse and a chimera.

Since Words are considered the great conduits of truth and knowledge, and we use them in conveying and receiving truths and reasoning about them, Locke proposes to consider wherein the certainty of real truths contained in propositions consists, and which universal propositions whose truth or falsehood we are capable of knowing with certainty. These tasks occupy him in chapters VI–VIII.

In chapter VI, Locke considers universal propositions about

substances. If we take the view that substances have a real essence that is unknown to us, then we will get no universal propositions that can be known with certainty. On the other hand, if we adopt Locke's view that essences and species are determined by the nominal essence, then our species terms will have a determinate significance, but we still won't get very many universal propositions. The main reason for this is that our knowledge of the co-existence of properties is largely limited to experience. In order to discover other qualities that co-exist with the combinations we experience, we would need to know 'their natural dependence; which in the primary Qualities, we can go but a very little way in; and in all their secondary Qualities, we can discover no connection at all' (IV. VI. 7. 18–20.: 582). The reason why we cannot find these natural dependences is that we don't know the real constitution which the secondary qualities depend on, and even if we did our knowledge would be limited to the experience we have, because we cannot even conceive of the connection between any modification of primary qualities and our ideas of secondary qualities. Therefore, Locke tells us, 'there are very few general Propositions to be made concerning Substances, which can carry with them *undoubted Certainty*' (IV. VI. 7. 27–29.: 582). In sections 8 and 9 Locke uses the example of gold to illustrate these points, and he continues to use that example into sections 10 and 11 to show that without knowing the necessary co-existence of properties, there are very few universal propositions about substances that we can know with certainty.

In section 11 Locke notes that the more ideas of qualities we include in our complex idea of a substance, the more precise and determinate the meaning of that word becomes; but the inclusion of more ideas of qualities does nothing to increase the universal certainty of propositions about other qualities not contained in our complex idea. What we need to know about substances is which properties necessarily co-exist or are repugnant to one another. If we could begin by knowing the real constitution of gold and what constitutes its qualities and what texture makes it, for example, malleable, fused and fixed, we would do much better in this regard. But this is not our situation. All that can be said is that if someone could discover the necessary co-existence or repugnancy of any set of properties of gold or any other substance, they would then be in a position to make universal propositions about that substance that would be as certain as any mathematical proposition. Locke remarks that if we had the ideas of how the real constitution of substances actually produce the sensible qualities we find in them, and how those sensible qualities flowed from the real constitution, we would not need the existence of gold or experiments on it. We could deduce from our ideas just what properties would co-exist or be repugnant to that substance just as we do in mathematics. But we are not even close to being in such a state.

In a passage remarkable for its grandeur of vision and its insistence on the interconnected character of everything in the universe, Locke goes on to argue for the importance of a knowledge of co-existence of properties. He begins by noting the unobvious connections between things that we usually take to be independent existences. Without the influence of other bodies, gold and water might lose characteristics that we think of as essential to them. Without air to breathe most living things would quickly die. Were the earth a little closer or farther away from the sun most of the animals would perish. Locke goes on to note that when we look at the constitution of a fly or an elephant, we completely fail to find an explanation of the qualities and powers we find in them. He conjectures that to understand these aright we might have to look 'not only beyond this our Earth and Atmosphere, even beyond the Sun, or the remotest Star our Eyes have yet discovered. For how much the Being and Operations of particular Substances in this our Globe, depend on causes utterly beyond our view, is impossible for us to determine' (IV. VI. 11. 8–12.: 587). It is possible, Locke continues, that the great parts and wheels of the structure of the universe may be so interconnected that a slight change in a star vastly removed from us might cause things in this our mansion to put on quite a different face or cease to exist. This passage does not fit very well with the picture of Locke the physical and social atomist who does not see the connections among things.

These considerations, Locke tells us, show how unlikely it is that we will ever discover the real essences of things, so we should not be surprised that our general knowledge of substances is very narrow and scanty. Things are even worse with our ideas of spirits than they are with material substances. We have no idea how they think or how they move bodies, and if we examine our ideas of bodies, things are only likely to get worse in this regard (IV. VI. 14. 19–26.: 589).

Locke goes on to point out that even with as familiar a substance as 'man', our ability to make firm generalizations about this kind of substance is strictly limited by our ignorance of the real constitution from which its qualities and powers flow. Thus, such propositions as 'All men sleep by intervals'; that 'No man can be nourished by wood or stones'; or that 'All men will be poisoned by hemlock' are at best probable. 'We must in these and the like appeal to Trial in particular subjects, which can reach but a little way' (IV. VI. 15. 13–14.: 590). Locke concludes this chapter by noting that we can only have certainty about general propositions when we can discover the agreements and disagreements of the ideas these propositions express. Experiment and observation will only give us knowledge of particulars. So ' 'Tis the contemplation of our own abstract *Ideas*, that alone is able to afford us general knowledge' (IV. VI. 16. 4–5.: 591).

Questions

22. Why does the problem of the reality of knowledge extend to truth?
23. How might he give the same answer to the problem about truth raised in IV. V. 7 as the one he gave about knowledge in the previous chapter? How does adding the distinction between verbal and real truths extend that answer?
24. Why does Locke take up the nature of universal propositions?
25. What universal propositions about substances does he think are possible? What are the chief limits on our making such propositions?

Maxims and tautologies

Chapters VII and VIII deal with matters which are not useful for knowledge, but which the scholastics treat as important. In particular, Locke treats of general maxims or axioms in chapter VII and trifling propositions in chapter VIII.

In the chapter on maxims, Locke returns to a subject that first appeared in Book I. Maxims, or axioms, are supposed to be first principles of the sciences. If they are not innate, as Locke argues they are not in Book I, then they are at least self-evident general truths. But, Locke says, there are many more truths besides these that are self-evident. To show these he examines the truths we get from the four types of agreement or disagreement listed in IV. II: identity, co-existence, relations and real existence. For any determinate idea, it is a self-evident truth that it is identical with itself and it is also self-evident that it is different from any other determinate idea. It does not matter in this case whether the ideas be more or less general or comprehensive. In terms of the co-existence of properties, we have very little intuitive knowledge and therefore very few self-evident truths. The only one Locke mentions is that '*Two bodies cannot be in the same place*' (IV. VII. 5. 16–17.: 594). As to relations, the axioms of mathematics, which are modal truths, supply a number of self-evident truths. But Locke claims that there are vastly more specific examples that have a clearer self-evidence than the general truths. Finally, in respect to real existence, we have intuitive self-evident knowledge of our own existence and demonstrative knowledge of the existence of God. Beyond that, we have no self-evident knowledge of the existence of things. So there are no maxims about the real existence of things.

In sections 8–10, Locke discusses the influence of these maxims on the other parts of our knowledge. He claims that the received opinion is that they are '*ex praecognitis, et praeconcesis* – "from what are known and conceded beforehand"' (IV. VII. 8. 3–4.: 595. See also Glossary in the *Essay*: 838). Locke claims that *praecognita* means that these axioms are known before others and that the other parts of knowledge depend on them. Locke denies that either of these claims are true. First, maxims like '*tis impossible for the same thing to be and not to be*' are generalizations from particular instances and not things from which the truth of particular instances are deduced. Second, these maxims are not the foundation of all our knowledge, since there are many other self-evident truths. At this point Locke makes a famous remark about the difficulties of abstraction. He points out that it is more difficult to make general ideas than one might think. Take, for example, the abstract idea of a triangle. Locke asks: 'Does it not require some pains and skill to form the *general Idea of a Triangle* ... for it must be neither Oblique, nor Rectangle, neither Equilateral, Equicrural, nor Scaleneon; but all and none of these at once' (IV. VII. 9. 4–9.: 596). Berkeley was later to seize on this account of abstraction to argue that it is incoherent. There are more charitable readings than the one Berkeley adopted. Leaving this aside, Locke's point is simply that dealing with abstractions is not as easy as it might look and that maxims are not the truths known to the mind before all others.

In fact, there are many other self-evident truths that provide a basis for inference.

In sections 11 and 12 Locke considers what maxims are useful for and what they are not useful for. In section 12 he remarks that where we do not have determinate ideas, that is, where our notions are 'wrong, loose or unsteady,' maxims not only do not help us, they will confirm our mistakes and serve to prove contradictions (IV. VII. 12. 3.: 604).

In section 15 Locke claims that in cases where we clearly know what our words mean, and no proof is required, maxims can be used without danger. On the other hand, in cases where we are using names of substances in proofs, the maxims ' "*Whatever is is*," and " '*tis impossible for the same thing to be and not to be*" – there they are of infinite danger and most commonly make Men receive Falsehood for Manifest Truth, and Uncertainty for Demonstration whereupon follows Errour, Obstinacy, and all the Mischiefs that can happen from False Reasoning' (IV. VII. 15. 14–17.: 606). The example of this claim that Locke gives in 16–18 involves the term 'man'. Locke gives three different inadequate definitions of man and shows the dangerous consequences that follow from using maxims together with these inadequate definitions to make proofs. The first inadequate definition is that of a child who thinks that the visible complex of apparent qualities, including white or flesh-colour, in England makes the idea of man. A child with such an idea can prove to you, using his inadequate definition and the maxim that ' '*tis impossible for the same thing to be and not to be*', that a Negro is not a man 'because White colour was one of the constant simple *Ideas* of the complex *Idea* he called *Man*' (IV. VII. 16. 6–8.: 607). Locke points out that the assurance such a child would have does not come from the maxim, but from the self-evident truth that black is not white. Some scholars have tried to twist this example to draw the conclusion that Locke endorses the conclusion that a Negro is not a man. No such reading is credible. Locke is arguing that using maxims in proofs along with inadequate definitions is dangerous; the example shows just such a danger (Uzgalis, 2002: 84–5).

Most of chapter VIII is taken up with a discussion of uninformative identity statements such as 'gold is gold'. Locke's point is that while the scholastics claim that such identity sentences are important, they in fact tell us nothing at all about the world. But what about informative identity sentences, such as 'the morning star is the evening star'? At IV. VIII. 3. 3–10.: 612, Locke notes that others use identity to refer to propositions 'wherein the same term is not affirmed of itself' and basically says that this is not how he is using the term identical propositions. If Locke is indeed rejecting the notion of informative identity statements, he is missing one of the more useful tools for dealing with the mind/body problem.

Locke next turns to cases where a part of an idea is predicated of the whole, as when we say that man is an animal. Locke thinks that such sentences are uninformative to one who knows what a man is. Such sentences are only useful in cases where the person being spoken to does not know the whole. In section 8 Locke suggests that, in reference to substances, if such truths are certain they are trifling, and if they are instructive 'are uncertain, and such as we can have no knowledge of their real Truth, how much soever constant Observation and Analogy may assist our Judgments in guessing' (IV. VIII. 8. 9–11.: 615). Locke claims that because this is so, people are able to write discourses using the 'relative Significations' and 'relative Definitions' of substantial beings that allows them to make propositions that can be affirmed or denied based on these definitions and significations and 'all this, without any knowledge of the Nature or Reality of Things existing without us' (IV. VIII. 9. 19–20.: 615). This is characteristic of many 'Books of Metaphysics, School-Divinity, and some sort of natural philosophy' (IV. VIII. 9. 29–30.: 615).

Questions

26. What are Locke's initial objections to the claim that maxims are the first principles of the sciences?
27. What are Locke's objections to the claim that maxims are known 'ex praecognitis, et praeconcesis'?
28. Under what conditions can maxims be used without danger?
29. Under what conditions is using maxims dangerous? What is the example that Locke gives?
30. In chapter VIII, why does Locke claim that identity statements are not useful?

Real existence

In chapters IX through X in Book IV Locke returns to issues about knowledge of real existence for the third time and along by now familiar lines. Chapter IX has to do with our knowledge of our own existence, X about the existence of God and XI about our knowledge of other things.

In chapter IX Locke explicitly endorses the *cogito*, Descartes' famous 'I think therefore I exist'. It should be clear by now that while Locke has no problem with the existence of the self, he is completely unwilling to follow Descartes' next step in the *Meditations* where he claims to establish that his essence is to be a thinking thing (Descartes: 80–3).

In chapter X Locke gives a proof for the existence of God that differs in important ways from the proof that Descartes gives in 'Meditation III'. It does not depend on an innate idea of God. Rather, Locke's proof depends on the impossibility of insensible and unthinking matter producing sense and thought. Since we are creatures that have sense and thought, Locke holds that there must be some eternal being that has these powers and capacities; otherwise you would have something arising from nothing. Locke defends his proof against various objections, mainly those from materialists.

In chapter XI Locke turns to our knowledge of the real existence of material things. He claims that while we have intuitive knowledge of our own existence and demonstrative knowledge of God's existence, we only know about the existence of other things through sensation. We may not know how perception works, but that does not take away from the certainty that perception tells us of the qualities that exist in the material world. If someone were sceptical enough to doubt the existence of the things she senses, she would be in no position to deal on the most basic level with the world. As Locke says: 'At least, he that can doubt so far, (whatever he may have within his own Thoughts) will never have any Controversie with me; since he can never be sure that I say anything contrary to his Opinion' (IV. XI. 3. 22–25.: 631). Locke goes on to give a number of reasons why 'the Confidence that our Faculties do not herein deceive us, is the greatest Assurance we are capable of, concerning the Existence of material Beings' (IV. XI. 3. 29–31.: 631). These reasons include that I can use material objects to cause myself pleasure and pain; that our faculties are necessary for knowledge or even a conception of knowledge; that it is plain that our perceptions are produced in us by exterior causes, because there are times when I cannot control the production of ideas; that many of these ideas are produced in us with pain that afterwards we cannot feel; that the senses in various cases bear witness to each other's reports. All of these reasons combined amount to an inference to the best explanation. The presence of material objects outside us best explains the fact that I can use them to cause myself pleasure or pain. Locke also answers the sceptic by claiming that while our faculties may not be suited to the full and perfect comprehension of material objects, leaving no doubts or scruples, they are sufficient for our preservation. It is also the case that: 'Such an assurance of the existence of Things without us, is sufficient to direct us in attaining the Good and avoiding the Evil, which is caused by them, which is the important concernment we have of being acquainted with them' (IV. XI. 8. 9–12.: 635). Locke goes on to say that the reason why it is only present perception that gives us certainty of the existence of the material things we perceive at that time is that once we no longer perceive a thing, it could cease to exist. Thus, it is not because of worries about sceptical arguments but because of facts about the world and perception that Locke asserts that our knowledge of sensible things is sharply limited. Memory also provides us with a guarantee that things we previously perceived really did exist when we perceived them. We only have faith and not knowledge that finite spirits exist, for we do not perceive them.

Questions

31. In dealing with the real existence of material things, Locke, in effect, suggests that radical scepticism is incoherent. What is the argument for this conclusion?
32. How adequate do you find Locke's inference to the best explanation resolution of the problem of real existence?

The improvement of our knowledge

In chapter XII of Book IV Locke concludes his discussion of knowledge by considering how our knowledge could be improved. He returns once again to the topic of maxims. What the scholastics had suggested was a model of the sciences that is derived from mathematics. The model suggests that all knowledge begins from certain principles or axioms or maxims and that the rest of knowledge is then derived from these principles. Locke says that given the enormous success of mathematics, it is easy to understand why such a model would be adopted. Still, from the discussion of maxims in Book I and in Book IV, chapter VII, we already know that Locke rejects this model. The principles are not known first, nor is our knowledge derived from them. Locke's discussion of the first principles of science in this section is reminiscent of the discussion about the method of discovery or analysis as opposed to the method of presentation or synthesis in Euclid and the other ancient mathematicians whom European mathematicians had engaged with in late sixteenth and early seventeenth century. Locke suggests that one fundamental problem is that we are likely to accept the principles without examining them and that when we do so we are likely to be led into error or confirmed in our mistakes. But, how are we supposed to tell the good ones from the bad ones? Locke argues that what we need to do is to '*fix in our Minds clear, distinct, and complete* Ideas, as far as they are to be had, *and annex to them proper and constant* Names' (IV. XII. 6. 30–33.: 642). Then we need to note the agreement and disagreement of these ideas and thus, without any principles, we may 'get more clear and true Knowledge, by the conduct of this one Rule, than by taking up Principles, and thereby putting our Minds into the Disposal of others' (IV. XII. 6. 35–2.: 642–3). Locke thinks that we can follow the mathematicians in this way of proceeding in the art of finding proofs, at least where we know the real essences of things. This led him to the suggestion advanced earlier that it might be possible to have a demonstrative science of morality.

With respect to our knowledge of substances, where we do not know their real essences we must proceed in a quite contrary way. Here reasoning about relations will do us very little good. Rather, we are going to have to depend on experience to teach us what properties co-exist with one another. But this will not get us very far, because there is no necessary connection between the properties whose co-existence we discover in this way. So, inductive reasoning in the absence of knowledge of the real essence of substances has little force. And while Locke admits that someone who has been accustomed to engage in rational and regular experiments will do better at understanding the nature of bodies, and will make better conjectures about what their unknown properties are, than someone who has not done this, this way of improving our knowledge of substances by 'Experience and History, which is all that the weakness of our Faculties in this state of *Mediocrity*, which we are in this World, can attain to, makes me suspect, that natural philosophy is not capable of being made a Science' (IV. XII. 10. 25–29.: 645). So what are we to make of this?

It is clear what Locke makes of it. In the next section he remarks that while the limits of our faculties in reaching the real essence and internal fabric of bodies makes us unfitted for making natural philosophy a science, we have no trouble determining our own existence and that of God. This suggests that 'our proper Imployment lies in those Enquiries, and in that sort of Knowledge, which is most suited to our natural Capacities, and carries in it our greatest interest, i.e. the condition of our Eternal Estate' (IV. XII. 11. 9–12.: 646). Locke goes on to claim that '*Morality is the proper Science and Business of Mankind in general* (who are both concerned and fitted out to search out their *Summum Bonum*)' (IV. XII. 11. 12–13.: 646). He does not object to some men pursuing the arts that relate to nature and are intended for their own subsistence and the common use of mankind. Things like the discovery of iron make a huge difference in the quality of human life. So Locke does not want to be thought of as discouraging the study of nature, which has produced such notable inventions as the compass, the printing press and quinine, that are more useful in supplying useful commodities and saving lives than the production of hospitals and colleges. Adopting hypotheses to explain certain phenomena of nature can both assist the memory and direct us to new discoveries. But we need to be cautious in adopting hypotheses. We need to examine carefully the phenomena we want to explain. We need to make sure that while our hypothesis explains, it does not conflict with some other relevant phenomenon. Locke does not want us to expect too much from the study of nature and above all to avoid the methods that the scholastics had introduced, and that he had earlier rejected.

Questions

33. Locke rejects Euclidian mathematics as a model for science. What is this model? What were the plausible reasons for the scholastics to adopt it? Why does he think we should reject it?

34. What is the alternative model that Locke proposes? In what way does his new model follow the procedures of the mathematicians?

35. What are the limitations on our abilities to know material substances and what does Locke conclude from this?

Knowledge and probability

Knowledge involves the seeing of the agreement or disagreement of our ideas. What then is probability and how does it relate to knowledge? Locke writes:

> The Understanding Faculties being given to Man, not barely for Speculation, but also for the Conduct of his Life, Man would be at a great loss, if he had nothing to direct him, but what has the Certainty of true Knowledge ... Therefore, as God has set some Things in broad day-light; as he has given us some certain Knowledge ... So in the greater part of our Concernment, he has afforded us only the twilight, as I may say so, of Probability, suitable, I presume, to that State of Mediocrity and Probationership, he has been pleased to place us in here, wherein to check our over-confidence and presumption, we might by every day's Experience be made sensible of our short sightedness and liableness to Error ... (IV. XIV. sections 1 & 2: 652)

So apart from the few important things that we can know for certain – such as the existence of ourselves and God, the general nature of mathematics and morality – for the most part we must lead our lives without knowledge. What then is probability? Locke writes:

> As Demonstration is the shewing of the Agreement or Disagreement of two *Ideas*, by the intervention of one or more Proofs, which have a constant, immutable, and visible connexion one with another: so *Probability* is nothing but the appearance of such an Agreement or Disagreement, by the intervention of Proofs, whose connexion is not constant and immutable, or at least is not perceived to be so, but is or appears, for the most part to be so, and is enough to induce the Mind to *judge* the Proposition to be true, or false, rather than the contrary. (IV. XV. 1.: 654)

Probable reasoning, on this account, is similar in certain ways to the demonstrative reasoning that produces knowledge, but also different in certain crucial respects. Locke's account of demonstrative knowledge provides a model for his account of probability. So, the fundamental principle of rational enquiry, that one should proportion assent to a proposition to the evidence for that proposition, holds in both realms. Just as Locke makes a distinction between actual and habitual knowledge, he makes a similar distinction about beliefs and probability (IV. XVI. 1. 2–18.: 658). It is an argument that provides evidence that leads the mind to judge a proposition as true or false, but without a guarantee that the judgement is correct. This kind of probable judgement comes in degrees, ranging from near demonstrations and certainty, through the unlikely and improbable, to the nearly impossible. It is correlated with degrees of assent ranging from full assurance down to conjecture, doubt and distrust.

The new science of mathematical probability had come into being on the Continent just around the time that Locke was writing the *Essay*. His account of probability, however, shows little or no awareness of mathematical probability. Rather, it reflects an older tradition that treated testimony as probable reasoning. Given that Locke's aim, above all, is to discuss what degree of assent we should give to various religious propositions, the older conception of probability very likely serves his purposes best. Thus, when Locke comes to describe the grounds for probability, he cites the conformity of the proposition to our knowledge, observation and experience, and the testimony of others who are reporting their observation and experience. Concerning the latter, we must consider the number of witnesses, their integrity, their skill in observation, counter-testimony and so on (IV. XV. 5. 4–10.: 656). In judging rationally how far to assent to a probable proposition, these are the relevant considerations that the mind should review. We should, Locke also suggests, be tolerant of differing opinions as we have more reason to retain the opinions we have than to give them up to strangers or adversaries who may well have some interest in our doing so (IV. XVI. 4. 30–6.: 659–60).

Locke distinguishes two sorts of probable proposition. The first of these is associated with particular existences or matters of fact; the second is beyond the testimony of the senses. Matters of fact are open to observation and experience, and so all of the tests are available to us for determining rational assent to propositions about them. Things are quite otherwise with matters that are beyond the testimony of the senses. These include the knowledge of finite immaterial spirits such as angels or things such as atoms that are too small to be seen, or the plants, animals or inhabitants of other planets that are beyond our range of sensation, because of their distance from us. Concerning this latter category, Locke says we must depend on analogy as the only aid for our reasoning. He writes: 'Thus the observing that the bare rubbing of two bodies violently one upon the other, produce heat, and very often fire it self, we have reason to think, that what we call Heat and Fire consist of the violent agitation of the imperceptible minute parts of the burning matter' (IV. XVI. 12.: 665–6). We reason about angels again by analogy; considering the Great Chain of Being, we figure that while we have no experience of angels, the ranks of species above us is likely as numerous as that below, of which we do have experience. This reasoning is, however, only probable.

Questions

36. What is the distinction between knowledge and probability? If we were determined to stick with only things we know for certain, how does Locke think we would fare in the conduct of life? (See chapter XIV.)
37. Why might the older conception of probability be more useful for Locke's purposes than the new conception of mathematical probability that was coming into being as Locke was writing *An Essay Concerning Human Understanding*?
38. What are the two sorts of probable propositions?

Reason, faith and enthusiasm

The late seventeenth century in Britain saw the culmination of a movement towards rational religion that encompassed many competing groups, from the Anglican Latitudinarians to some Dissenters to the Deists. Locke's account of the epistemology of religion in chapters XVIII through XX of *An Essay Concerning Human Understanding* is an application to religion of the account of knowledge and probability developed in the first seventeen chapters of Book IV. It is worth recalling that James Tyrrell reported that the original impetus for the writing of the *Essay* was difficulties raised in a discussion about morality and revealed religion. Locke claims that there are truths above reason, but none contrary to reason. So, it is reason that determines what counts as genuine or false revelation. To claim that faith can do without reason is what Locke calls enthusiasm and amounts to abandoning the principle that one should proportion assent to a proposition to the evidence for it, all the evidence being considered. To give up this principle is to give up the love of truth. Locke's account of the epistemology of religion is, then, one of the most notable expositions of rational religion in the history of religious thought.

In Book IV, chapters XVII through XX, Locke deals with the nature of reason, the relation of reason to faith and the nature of enthusiasm. Locke remarks that all sects make use of reason as far as they can. It is only when this fails them that they have recourse to faith and claim that what is revealed is above reason. But he adds: 'And I do not see how they can argue with anyone or even convince a gainsayer who uses the same plea, without setting down strict boundaries between faith and reason' (IV. XVIII. 2.: 689). Locke then defines reason as 'the discovery of the certainty or probability of such propositions or truths, which the mind arrives at by deduction made from such ideas, as it has got by the use of its natural faculties; viz, by the use of sensation or reflection' (IV. XVIII. 2.: 689). Faith, on the other hand, is assent to any proposition 'upon the credit of the proposer, as coming from God, in some extraordinary way of communication'. So we have faith in what is disclosed by revelation and which cannot be discovered by reason. Locke also distinguishes between the original revelation by God to some person, and traditional revelation which is the original revelation 'delivered over to others in Words, and the ordinary ways of our conveying our Conceptions one to another' (IV. XVIII. 3. 22–23.: 690).

Locke makes the point that some things could be discovered both by reason and by revelation. So God could reveal the propositions of Euclid's geometry, or they could be discovered by reason. In such cases there would be little use for faith. Traditional revelation can never produce as much certainty as the contemplation of the agreement or disagreement of our own ideas (IV. XVIII. 4. 26–1.: 690–1). Similarly revelations about matters of fact do not produce as much certainty as having the experience oneself. Revelation, then, cannot contradict what we know to be true. If it could, it would undermine the trustworthiness of all our faculties. This would be a disastrous result (IV. XVIII. 5. 11–19.: 692). Revelation comes into its own when we have few or no ideas for reason to contradict or confirm; for example, 'that Part of the Angels rebelled against GOD, and thereby lost their first happy state: and that the dead shall rise, and live again: These and the like, being Beyond the Discovery of Reason, are purely matters of Faith; with which Reason has nothing to do' (IV. XVIII. 7. 10–14.: 694). Still, reason does have a crucial role to play in respect to revelation. Locke writes:

> Because the Mind, not being certain of the Truth of that it evidently does not know, but only yielding to the Probability that appears to it, is bound to give up its assent to such Testimony, which, it is satisfied, comes from one who cannot err, and will not deceive. But yet, it still belongs to Reason, to judge of the truth of its being a Revelation, and of the significance of the Words, wherein it is delivered. (IV. XVIII. 8. 20–34.: 694)

So, in respect of the crucial question of how we are to know whether a revelation is genuine, we are supposed to use reason and the canons of probability to judge. Locke claims that if the boundaries between faith and reason are not clearly marked, then there will be no place for reason in religion and one then gets all the 'extravagant Opinions and Ceremonies, that are to be found in the several Religions of the World' (IV. XVIII. 11. 12–13.: 696).

In the fourth edition of the *Essay* Locke added a chapter on enthusiasm. Should one accept revelation without using reason to judge whether or not it is genuine revelation, one gets what Locke calls a third principle of assent besides reason and revelation, namely enthusiasm. Enthusiasm is a vain or unfounded confidence in divine favour or communication. It implies that there is no need to use reason to judge whether or not such favour or communication is genuine. Clearly when such communications are not genuine they are 'the ungrounded Fancies of a Man's own Brain' (IV. XIX. 3. 22–23.: 698). Locke describes enthusiasts as people who either have a mix of melancholy and devotion or who consider themselves among God's chosen people. These people flatter themselves that they have an immediate relationship with the deity. Their minds being thus prepared 'whatever groundless Opinion comes to settle itself strongly upon their Fancies, is an illumination from the Spirit of God' and any odd action they may do is 'a call or direction from Heaven, and must be obeyed' (IV. XIX. 6. 18–21.: 699). This kind of enthusiasm was characteristic of Protestant extremists of the English Civil War era. Locke was not alone in rejecting enthusiasm, but he rejects it in the strongest terms. Enthusiasm violates the fundamental principle by which the understanding operates: that assent should be proportioned to the evidence. To abandon that fundamental principle would be catastrophic (see IV. XVIII. 5. 19–24.: 691–2 and IV. XIX. 1. 10–21.: 697). This is a point that Locke also makes in *Of the Conduct of the Understanding* (Locke, 1823, Vol. III: 203–89) and *The Reasonableness of Christianity* (Locke, 1999), as well as here in the *Essay*. He wants each of us to use our understanding to search after truth; to engage in such a search is the road to freedom and maturity.

Of enthusiasts, those who would abandon reason and claim to know on the basis of faith alone, Locke writes: 'he that takes away Reason to make way for Revelation, puts out the Light of both, and does much what the same, as if he would perswade a Man to put out his eyes, the better to receive the remote Light of an invisible Star by a Telescope' (IV. XIX. 4. 31–35.: 698). Rather than engage in the tedious labour required to reason correctly, enthusiasts persuade themselves that they are possessed of immediate revelation, without having to use reason to judge the veracity of their revelation. This leads to 'odd Opinions and extravagant actions to be found in several Religions of the World' (IV. XVIII. II. 12–13.: 696). Thus, Locke strongly rejects any attempt to make legitimate the principle of inward persuasion not judged by reason.

Questions

39. What is Locke's account of reason?
40. Under what conditions do religious sects appeal to reason?
41. What are things above or beyond reason?
42. What is the distinction between original and traditional revelation?
43. What is the relation between faith and revelation?
44. What, on Locke's view, is the relation between reason and traditional revelation? Could traditional revelation overrule reason? Why or why not?
45. What is enthusiasm? How is it different from having faith?
46. Why does Locke think that enthusiasm is catastrophic for human understanding?

47. In what ways does Locke's account of religion depend on the views of knowledge and probability developed previously in Book IV?

Wrong assent

In chapter XX Locke talks more generally of the causes of error. He thinks that while the causes of error or wrong assent are many, this multitude of causes can be subsumed under four general causes: not having proofs, an inability to use proofs, not having the will to use them and having a wrong measure of probability.

In explaining the first general cause of error, Locke says that he does not mean by not having proofs simply those cases where there are no proofs. Rather, he means to include those cases where people do not have the time and opportunity to find those proofs that already exist, or do not have 'the Convenience and Opportunity to make Experiments and Observations themselves, tending to the Proof of any Proposition; nor likewise the Convenience to enquire into, and Collect the Testimony of Others' (IV. XX. 2. 3–6.: 707). Those in this situation include the greatest part of mankind. The opportunities to learn tend to be as narrow as one's fortune. A man who drudges all his life in some laborious trade is as likely to know as much about what is going on in the world as a pack-horse who is driven back and forth in a narrow lane knows of the geography of the country. Still, Locke says, even those in this condition do not want to leave their greatest concernment, their happiness or misery, to the chance of where they were born and leave themselves in the power of 'the current Opinions and licensed Guides of every Country' when it is apparent that there is considerable difference of opinion between guides and countries (IV. XX. 3. 1–2.: 708). Locke thinks that even people who labour most of the time have the faculties and can find the time to enquire about such important religious truths. This can either be taken as a good Protestant point about one's responsibility for one's own salvation, or perhaps more radically as requiring the study of comparative religion; what shortly came to be called free thinking.

Conclusion: the division of the sciences

Having completed his discussion of religious truths, the *Essay* ends rather abruptly with a brief chapter on the division of the sciences. Locke claims that the nature of bodies and minds constitutes one branch of science. He sees this as an enlarged sense of natural philosophy. Secondly, there is the realm of human conduct in which what we need is the 'Skill of Right applying our own Powers and Actions, for the Attainment of things good and useful' (IV. XXI. 3. 18–19.: 720). Ethics is most important here as it is the 'seeking out of those Rules and Measures of humane Action, which lead to Happiness, and the Means to practise them' (IV. XXI. 3. 20–23.: 720). Finally, there is the doctrine of signs 'the business whereof, is to consider the nature of Signs, the Mind makes use of for the Understanding of Things, or conveying its Knowledge to others' (IV. XXI. 4. 27–29.: 720). This involves an investigation of ideas and words that Locke calls logic or critique. Locke claims that each of these provinces of knowledge is completely different from the others and so this represents 'the first and most general, as well as natural division of the Objects of the Understanding' (IV. XXI. 5. 16–17.: 721).

Questions

48. What are Locke's views on the duty of ordinary people to search for religious truths?
49. What are the three different kinds of sciences in Locke's division of sciences, and how do they reflect the structure of *An Essay Concerning Human Understanding*?

CHAPTER 4

RECEPTION AND INFLUENCE

Locke's *An Essay Concerning Human Understanding* was both popular and controversial from the first publication of the 92-page summary in the *Bibliotheque universelle et historique* for January through March 1688 and throughout the first half of the eighteenth century. Hans Aarsleff remarks that Locke 'is the most influential philosopher of modern times' (Aarsleff, 1994: 252). He notes that besides initiating the vigorous tradition known as British empiricism, Locke's influence reached far beyond the limits of the traditional discipline of philosophy. 'His influence in the history of thought, on the way we think about ourselves and our relation to the world we live in, to God, nature and society, has been immense' (Aarsleff, 1994: 252). Locke influenced not only such philosophers as Berkeley and Hume, but also Voltaire, Condiallac, Jonathan Edwards, Dr Johnson, Jonathan Swift and Laurence Sterne. The work was appreciated both in England and on the Continent, especially in the first half of the eighteenth century. We should note the influence of some of the particular topics and themes in the *Essay*.

We might begin with the polemic in Book I against innate ideas. By the first years of the eighteenth century Locke's arguments against innate principles and innate ideas had largely prevailed (Yolton, 1996: 25). The success of Locke's polemic against innate ideas was one of the *Essay*'s clear early achievements. We should recall, however, that Locke's rejection of innate ideas was part of his larger rejection of the scholastic model of science, as derived by deduction from first principles, in favour of empirical enquiry. The proposed change in the way we conceive knowledge and enquiry was also largely successful, and the *Essay* played a significant role in this change, by providing a sustained and enormously influential defence of empiricism and empirical enquiry.

Locke's rejection of innate ideas implies the autonomy of the individual in searching for the truth and in determining what acts to do or refrain from doing. The radical nature of Locke's attacks on political, epistemic and religious authority are difficult for us to grasp today (Aarsleff, 1994: 252). The period in which Locke wrote was filled with religious and political oppression, which often forced people to leave their homes and become refugees. England was hardly exempt from these problems as Locke's own life illustrates.

A number of commentators have noted that the success of Locke's *Essay* in part turned on the fact that in barely concealed form it dealt with religious controversies of the day. One of Locke's most important early critics was Bishop Edward Stillingfleet who suggested that Locke's ideas undermined important religious doctrines, such as the Trinity. Locke denied this, but we have good reason to conclude that he was an anti-Trinitarian, so it may well be that we should take these denials with a grain of salt. Deists in the late seventeenth and early eighteenth century adopted Locke's opinions about the role of reason in religion. The Deists rejected religious mysteries, including the Trinity, and insisted on a rational religion. John Toland's *Christianity not Mysterious*, which employed Locke's epistemological principles, was the most controversial of these. Its publication caused a strong reaction from more traditional religious thinkers, leading Locke to publish *The Reasonableness of Christianity* (Locke, 1999). By the middle of the eighteenth century the era of rational religion in Britain was coming to an end.

George Berkeley's attack on the causal theory of perception and on the distinction between primary and secondary qualities, as well as Locke's account of substance and abstraction, represented the beginning of an influential misinterpretation of the *Essay*. Berkeley, in effect, held that Locke's solution to the problem of real existence was inadequate because of the veil of perception problem explained above in the section on 'Resemblance and representative theories of perception'. Berkeley's radical solution was to reject the notion of matter as incoherent. British empiricism thus took an idealist turn. Berkeley's views led to Reid's rejection of 'the way of ideas' as having amongst its absurd consequences the rejection of the existence of the external world. This influential misinterpretation of Locke lived on well into the twentieth century and is perhaps not dead yet.

Locke's account of personal identity was genuinely revolutionary and one of his most striking contributions to philosophy. It too had religious implications. Conservative Anglicans rejected Locke's substitution of consciousness for substance as the bearer of personal identity. These included Bishop Stillingfleet, Samuel Clarke, Bishop Butler and George Berkeley. On the continent Leibniz had much the same reaction. But in spite of his critics, Locke's views on personal identity were influential and not just among philosophers and theologians.

Locke's example of a rational talking parrot which implied that 'person' might be a trans-species concept may have inspired Jonathan Swift's account of Gulliver's fourth voyage in which he encounters rational talking horses and irrational human beings. Swift and his friends went on to parody the debates in the early eighteenth century about personal identity in *The Memoirs of Scriblerius*, and Locke's account of personal identity went on to influence English literature in a variety of ways. Even among the philosophers and theologians, Locke's revolutionary account was regularly attacked and defended over the remainder of the eighteenth century and this debate was largely recapitulated in the twentieth century.

The extent of the influence that Locke's account of language has had over the centuries is a matter of scholarly debate. Norman Kretzmann holds that Locke's views, while not original, had a powerful influence on the Enlightenment view of the connection of words and ideas (Kretzmann: 123). Noam Chomsky, in *Cartesian Linguistics*, traces important ideas in linguistics back to Descartes and the school at Port Royal rather than Locke (Chomsky, 1966). This is largely a matter of the importance of nativism in Chomsky's thought. Hans Aarsleff, on the other hand, believes that Locke stands at the beginning of the developments that produced contemporary linguistics and argues that Chomsky's account is more polemical than historical (Aarsleff, 1982: 101–19).

Locke's account of the relation of real and nominal essences turned out to be wrong in important ways, and shows that he vastly underestimated the progress science would make. This is the most significant and far reaching mistake in the *Essay*, though given the state of science at the end of the seventeenth century it is quite understandable why Locke would make it. On the other hand, Locke's emphasis on the human origins of language and the making of language and classificatory systems for pragmatic purposes continues to inform even contemporary empiricist metaphysics. It is unclear to what extent these views may have contributed to the development of evolutionary thought in England, but they certainly could have played a role.

While Locke's critics tended to focus more on Book II than Book IV, perhaps the most controversial of Locke's claims was the passing remark in Book IV that it was just as possible that God had made fitly disposed matter capable of thinking as that he had conjoined an immaterial thinking substance with a body. Critics saw this as an expression of materialism and the debate over thinking matter continued through the bulk of the eighteenth century.

Locke's reputation declined significantly in the nineteenth century. Locke was identified with the thought of the philosophes and the encyclopedists who where held to be responsible for the French Revolution (Aarsleff, 1994: 278). Locke was identified as one of the false prophets of the eighteenth century. Fox Bourne's groundbreaking two-volume biography of Locke was published in the late nineteenth century, but failed to stimulate much interest in Locke's philosophy.

In the twentieth century Locke's reputation underwent a great revival that continues unabated into the twenty-first. The availability to Locke scholars of the Lovelace papers and the recognition that Locke needed to be read in his historical, religious, political and scientific context has provided much better insight into the development of the thought in the *Essay* than was possible earlier. The project of producing a new critical edition of all of Locke's works, begun by the Clarendon Press in 1972 with the Nidditch edition of the *Essay*, is now well under way.

BIBLIOGRAPHY

BOOKS

Aarsleff, Hans, *From Locke to Saussure: Essays on the Study of Language and Intellectual History*, Minnneapolis: University of Minnesota Press, 1982.

Ayers, Michael, *Locke: Epistemology and Ontology*, London: Routledge, 1991.

Berkeley, George, *Works*, A.C. Luce and T.E.Jessop (eds), 9 vols, London: T. Nelson, 1957.

Boyle, Robert, *The Works of the Honourable Robert Boyle*, Thomas Birch (ed.), 6 vols, facsimile reprint, Hildesheim: Georg Olms Verlagsbuch-handlung, 1966.

Chappell, Vere, (ed.), *The Cambridge Companion to Locke*, Cambridge: Cambridge University Press, 1994.

Chappell, Vere, (ed.), *Locke*, Oxford: Oxford University Press, 1998

Chomsky, Noam, *Syntactic Structures*, The Hague: Mouton, 1957.

Chomsky, Noam, *Cartesian Linguistics: A Chapter in the History of Rationalist Thought*, New York: Harper and Row, 1966.

Cudworth, Ralph, *The True Intellectual System of the Universe*, 1678 facsimile, Stuttgart: F. Fromman, 1964.

Descartes, René, *Selected Philosophical Writings*, John Cottingham, Robert Stoothoff and Douglas Murdoch (trans.), Cambridge: Cambridge University Press, 1988.

Fox, Christopher, *Locke and the Scriblerians: Identity and Consciousness in Early Eighteenth-Century Britain*, Berkeley: University of California Press, 1988.

Leibniz, Gottfried W., *New Essays Concerning Human Understanding*, Peter Remnant and Jonathan Bennett (trans. and eds), Cambridge: Cambridge University Press, 1996.

Locke, John, *The Works of John Locke*, 9 vols, London, 1823.

Locke, John, *An Essay Concerning Human Understanding*, Peter Nidditch (ed.), Oxford, Clarendon Press, 1972.

Locke, John, *The Second Treatise of Government*, C.B. Macpherson (ed.), Indianapolis: Hackett Publishing Co., 1980.

BIBLIOGRAPHY

Locke, John, *The Reasonableness of Christianity As Delivered in the Scriptures*, John C. Higgins-Biddle (ed.), Oxford, Clarendon Press, 1999.

Mackie, John L., *Problems from Locke*, Oxford: Clarendon Press, 1976.

Mandelbaum, Maurice, *Philosophy, Science and Sense Perception*, Baltimore: The Johns Hopkins Press, 1966.

Martin, Raymond and John Barresi, *Naturalization of the Soul: Self and Personal Identity in the Eighteenth Century*, London: Routledge, 2000.

Montaigne, Michel de, *An Apology for Raymond Sebond*, M.A. Screech (trans.), London: Penguin Books, 1987.

Oberhoff, Jürgen, *Hobbes's Theory of the Will*, Lanham, MD: Rowman and Littlefield, 2000.

Ryle, Gilbert, *The Concept of Mind*, New York, Barnes and Noble, 1949.

Yaffe, Gideon, *Liberty Worth the Name: Locke on Free Agency*, Princeton, NJ: Princeton University Press, 2000.

Yolton, John, *Locke and the Compass of Human Understanding*, Cambridge: Cambridge University Press, 1970.

Yolton, John, *Thinking Matter: Materialism in 18th Century Britain*, Minneapolis: University of Minnesota Press, 1983.

Yolton, John, *Locke and the Way of Ideas*, Bristol: Thoemmes Press, 1996.

ARTICLES

Aarsleff, Hans, 'Locke's Influence', in Chappell, 1994, pp. 252–89.

Atherton, Margaret, 'Locke and the Issue over Innateness', in Chappell, 1998, pp. 48–59.

Bouwsma, Oets Kolk, 'Descartes' Skepticism of the Senses', *Mind: A Quarterly Review of Philosophy*, 54 (1945) pp. 313–22.

Bouwsma, Oets Kolk, 'Descartes' Evil Genius', in Sesonske and Fleming (eds), *Meta-Meditations*, Belmont, CA: Wadsworth Publishing Co., 1967.

Bracken, Harry M., 'Essence, Accident and Race', in *Hermethena*, 16 (1973), pp. 81–96.

Guyer, Paul, 'Locke's Philosophy of Language', in Chappell, 1994, pp. 115–45.

Kretzmann, Norman, 'The Main Thesis of Locke's Semantic Theory' in Ian Tipton (ed.), *Locke on Human Understanding*, Oxford: Oxford University Press, 1977, pp. 123–40.

McCann, Edwin, 'Locke's Philosophy of Body' in Chappell, 1994.

Milton, John R., 'Locke's Life and Times', in Chappell, 1994, pp 5–25.

Uzgalis, William, 'The Anti-Essential Locke and Natural Kinds', *The Philosophical Quarterly*, 38 (152) (July 1988), pp. 330–40.

Uzgalis, William, 'Relative Identity and Locke's Principle of Individuation', *History of Philosophy Quarterly*, 7(3) (July 1990) pp. 283–97.

Uzgalis, William, ' "An Inconsistency not to be excused": On Locke and Racism', in *Philosophers on Race: Critical Essays*, Julie K. Ward and Tommy L. Lott (eds), Oxford: Blackwell, 2002, pp. 81–100.

Wilson, Robert, 'Locke's Primary Qualities', *Journal of the History of Philosophy*, 40(2) (2002), pp. 201–28.

INDEX